Plant Genetic Resources

A Conservation Imperative

AAAS Selected Symposia Series

 Published by Westview Press, Inc.
5500 Central Avenue, Boulder, Colorado

for the

 American Association for the Advancement of Science
1776 Massachusetts Ave., N.W., Washington, D.C.

Plant Genetic Resources

A Conservation Imperative

Edited by Christopher W. Yeatman, David Kafton, and Garrison Wilkes

AAAS Selected Symposium **87**

AAAS Selected Symposia Series

This book is based on a symposium that was held at the 1981 AAAS National
Annual Meeting in Toronto, Ontario, January 3-8. The symposium was sponsored
by AAAS Section G (Biology).

Published in 1984 in the United States of America by Westview Press, Inc.,
5500 Central Avenue, Boulder, Colorado 80301; Frederick A. Praeger,
Publisher

Library of Congress Catalog Card Number: 84-51723
ISBN: 0-8133-0129-7

Printed and bound in the United States of America

10 9 8 7 6 5 4 3 2 1

About the Book

The ability of plants to continue to feed, clothe, house, heat, and heal mankind is contingent on maintaining the genetic diversity of the vast--but shrinking--number of plant species in existence today. The genetic erosion of both wild and cultivated plants is alarming, and there is a special need to husband the genetic resources of the relatively few major crop species.

This volume reviews the history of crop-plant development, introduction, and conservation in North America, outlines some effective policies and strategies for dynamic genetic conservation in plants, particularly those of direct economic value, and examines a variety of problems in and opportunities for preservation and utilization of the irreplaceable genetic heritage in agriculture and forestry.

About the Series

The *AAAS Selected Symposia Series* was begun in 1977 to provide a means for more permanently recording and more widely disseminating some of the valuable material which is discussed at the AAAS Annual National Meetings. The volumes in this *Series* are based on symposia held at the Meetings which address topics of current and continuing significance, both within and among the sciences, and in the areas in which science and technology impact on public policy. The *Series* format is designed to provide for rapid dissemination of information, so the papers are not typeset but are reproduced directly from the camera-copy submitted by the authors. The papers are organized and edited by the symposium arrangers who then become the editors of the various volumes. Most papers published in this *Series* are original contributions which have not been previously published, although in some cases additional papers from other sources have been added by an editor to provide a more comprehensive view of a particular topic. Symposia may be reports of new research or reviews of established work, particularly work of an interdisciplinary nature, since the AAAS Annual Meetings typically embrace the full range of the sciences and their societal implications.

WILLIAM D. CAREY
Executive Officer
American Association for
the Advancement of Science

Contents

About the Editors and Authors.................... xi

Introduction: Global Heritage in
    Jeopardy-- *Christopher W. Yeatman*.................1

    Literature Cited   2

PART 1.   HISTORY AND POLICY DEVELOPMENT
           IN AGRICULTURE

1   History of Plant Introduction
    in the United States-- *Howard L. Hyland*..........5

    Prior to Formalized USDA
       Program (1898)   6
    Early Explorations (1898-1930)   8
    Activities Before, During and
       Shortly After World War II
       (1930-1948)   10
    USDA-States Cooperative Program
       (1948-1975)   10
    Bibliography   13

2   Plant Germplasm Policy-- *R. W. Hougas*...........15

    National Plant Germplasm System   17
    Documentation and Guidelines   26
    National Plant Genetic Resources
       Board   27
    Conclusion   28
    Literature Cited   29

3   Conservation of Gene Resources
    in the United States-- *William L. Brown* 31

    Current Programs   31

Discussion   33
Animal Germplasm   35
Microorganisms   37
Current and Future Needs   38
Summary   40
Literature Cited   40

4   The Canadian Plant Gene Resources
      Program-- *Roland Loiselle* 43

The Formal Recognition of the
   Importance of Plant Gene
   Resources in Canada   44
The Objectives of the Plant Gene
   Resources Program   44
Inventory of Plant Gene Resources   45
Crop Information Banks   48
Seed Preservation at the Plant
   Gene Resources Office   48
Clonal Repositories for Tree
   Fruit Germplasm   49
Cryopreservation of Plant Genetic
   Resources   50
Collecting Expeditions   51
National and International
   Exchanges of Genetic Resources   51
Conclusions   51
Literature Cited   52

PART 2.   GENETIC RESOURCES IN FOREST
          AND WILDLIFE MANAGEMENT

5   The California Gene Resource
      Conservation Program-- *David Kafton* 55

The California Program   55
Genetic Resource Management   57
Phase One of the California
   Program   60
Phase Two of the California
   Program   60
The Long Term California Program   62
Literature Cited   62

6   Native Plant Gene Conservation
      in British Columbia-- *Bristol Foster* 63

History   63
The Ecological Reserves Act   64
Establishing Ecological Reserves   65

Management of Reserves   67
Research   68
Conclusions   68
Acknowledgements   69
Literature Cited   69

7   Policies, Strategies and Means for
     Genetic Conservation in Forestry--
     Stanley L. Krugman 71

     Forest History and Practice   72
     Management Issues   73
     Management Strategies   74
     Literature Cited   77

8   Strategies for Gene Conservation
     in Forest Tree Breeding-- *Gene Namkoong* 79

     Some Salient Features of Forest
        Trees   79
     Conservation and Breeding Programs 82
     Population Structures   83
     Program Structures   86
     Literature Cited   87

PART 3.   GENETIC CONSERVATION IN
          BREEDING CROP-PLANTS

9   Utilization of Genetic Diversity
     in Crop Breeding--*Lyndon W. Kannenberg*..........93

     Crop Diversity   93
     Genetic Erosion   94
     Sources of Diversity   98
     New Breeding Approaches   99
     HOPE   101
     Conclusion   105
     Literature Cited   106

10   Gene Centers and Gene Utilization
     in American Agriculture-- *Jack R. Harlan* 111

     Introduction   111
     Before World War II   112
     After World War II   123
     References   126

11   Germplasm Conservation Toward the
     Year 2000: Potential for New Crops
     and Enhancement of Present Crops--
     Garrison Wilkes 131

Crop Plants are Domesticated
   Plants   136
Plant Genetic Resources   137
Conservation in Perpetuity   139
Undervalued Plant Genetic
   Resources   140
New and Potential Crops   142
Species Diversity in the
   Humid Tropics   145
Improving the Plants of the
   Humid Tropics and New Crops   146
The Value of Plants from the
   Tropics   147
Conclusion   160
Literature Cited   160

About the Editors and Authors

Christopher W. Yeatman *is project leader for tree genetics and breeding at Petawawa National Forestry Institute in Chalk River, Ontario. His research interests are the genetic management and improvement of commercial conifers used for reforestation in Canada, especially the genecology of jack pine. He is a member of the Panel of Experts on Forest Gene Resources for the United Nation's Food and Agriculture Organization.*

David Kafton *is executive director of the National Council on Gene Resources and co-author of their reports on the genetic resources of anadromous salmonids, barley, Douglas-fir, and the strawberry. He is involved in a broad range of activities aimed at furthering understanding and promoting support for the management, conservation, and use of gene resources.*

Garrison Wilkes, *a professor of biology at the University of Massachusetts in Boston, specializes in economic botany and the evolution under domestication of crop plants. He has published on crop plant germplasm and the origin and evolution of maize and its relatives and is president-elect of the Society for the Study of Economic Botany.*

William L. Brown *is chairman of Pioneer Hi-Bred International in Johnston, Iowa. His primary research interests are the evolution, breeding, and genetics of maize. He has written papers on genetic diversity and genetic vulnerability, germplasm conservation, use of exotic germplasm in cereal improvement, and races of maize in the West Indies. He is currently chairman of the National Research Council's Board on Agriculture.*

Bristol Foster *is director of the ecological reserves unit for the Ministry of Lands, Parks, and Housing in Victoria, British Columbia. His research concentrates on ecosystem*

*conservation and he has written articles on ecological reserves
and threatened species and habitats in Canada.*

Jack R. Harlan, *a professor of plant genetics in the
Department of Agronomy at the University of Illinois, Urbana,
specializes in plant exploration and crop evolution. His
publications cover a wide range of topics including the origins
of indigenous African agriculture and plant breeding and genetics in the People's Republic of China. He is a member of the
National Academy of Sciences and past president of the Crop
Science Society of America.*

R. W. Hougas *is professor of genetics in the Department
of Horticulture at the University of Wisconsin, Madison. He
has done extensive research on plant breeding and has written
more than forty scientific papers on interspecific hybridization and genetic studies of wild and cultivated potatoes. For
thirteen years he was the leader of the national potato germplasm program sponsored by the U.S. Department of Agriculture.*

Howard L. Hyland, *a plant introduction officer for twenty-
seven years, prepared plant inventories for the USDA Agricultural Research Service in Washington, D.C., until he recently
retired. His research interests are agronomy and crop breeding.*

Lyndon W. Kannenberg *is professor of crop science at the
University of Guelph in Guelph, Ontario. A specialist in corn
breeding and genetics, he has written more than thirty articles
on population genetics, plant breeding, and corn production.*

Stanley L. Krugman *is director of timber management research for the U.S. Forest Service in Washington, D.C. Plant
physiology and forest genetics are his specialties and he has
written a series of papers on both national and international
strategies for forest tree gene conservation.*

Roland Loiselle *has been head of the Central Office for
the Plant Gene Resources of Canada in Ottawa since it was
established in 1970 as part of the Canada Department of Agriculture. He is involved in many different programs involving
plant breeding, genetics, plant pathology, agronomy, and
statistics.*

Gene Namkoong *is a geneticist for the U.S. Forest Service
and professor of genetics and of forestry at North Carolina
State University, Raleigh. He is the author of over ninety
publications on evolution and breeding including* Introduction
to Quantitative Genetics in Forestry *(USDA and Castle House,
1981) and has served as consultant to the governments of
Canada and the Republic of Korea.*

Christopher W. Yeatman

Introduction:
Global Heritage in Jeopardy

The ability of plants to continue to feed, clothe, house, heat and heal mankind is contingent on maintaining their genetic diversity. It is as essential to meet future, unknown requirements as it is to develop and improve plants used in agriculture and forestry today. An accelerating rate of genetic erosion of both wild and cultivated plants is cause for alarm and must receive increased attention, both public and scientific. Once destroyed, genetic resources are lost forever, as is dramatically illustrated by species extinctions. Genetic conservation of wild plant and animal species and populations is properly a continuing concern of conservationists and biologists and was the subject of a recent symposium held in Washington, D.C. (Schoenewald-Cox et al. 1983). Society generally is less aware of the critical need to husband genetic resources of the relatively few major crop species which are the focus of this publication.

Germplasm resources in agriculture was the subject of a AAAS symposium held during the 1959 meeting in Chicago (Hodgson 1961). The present volume includes papers presented at three subsequent AAAS symposia in Boston, San Francisco and Toronto, in 1976, 1980 and 1981. They reflect a growing awareness that retention of genetic diversity is a condition for long-term survival (Frankel 1970) and they illustrate the development of concepts and means for sustaining and employing crop-plant genetic resources.

Domestication and breeding, combined with cultivation and intensive management, are at once a cause and a requirement of an escalating human population. As man narrows the genetic base of major crop plants of the world in the interests of improved efficiency, economy, quality and uniformity, he increases their vulnerability to adverse biological agents or environmental changes. New cultural

stresses, and opportunities, call for novel genetic solutions. These must be developed principally from existing
and known reserves of genetic variability. Such reserves
for agricultural plants are retained in landraces, cultivars
and breeding collections which are vulnerable to replacement, loss or neglect. Natural populations of forest and
forage species and wild relatives of domesticated species
are being reduced, eliminated or replaced. The rate and
scale of change has outstripped the capacity of ecosystems
to respond to the evolutionary forces of natural selection
and reproduction.

Genetic erosion is occurring on a global scale yet
genetic diversity is essential to continuing evolutionary
development, whether directed by man or by nature. Clearly,
it is neither possible, nor even desirable, to regenerate in
perpetuity samples of every existing breeding population,
genetic line, or clone. Needs must be analyzed carefully
and priorities set. The means to be applied are many and
diverse. Choices must be governed by knowledge of species
and their natural and managed cultural systems, and by
resources committed to this most vital aspect of biological
management.

The purpose here is to review the history of crop-plant
development and introduction in North America, to outline
effective policies and strategies required to implement
dynamic genetic conservation in plants, particularly those
of direct economic value, and to contrast the variety of
problems, opportunities and solutions in agriculture and
forestry. Much has been done by dedicated scientists, agri-
culturalists, foresters, naturalists and far-sighted politicians and bureaucrats. Succeeding generations must build on
this foundation in order to maintain the diversity of
genetic resources in every part of the globe. Past activity
has concentrated on collection, storage and preservation.
Additional emphasis must now be given to evaluation, documentation, publication, and utilization of this precious
genetic heritage if it is to be adequately appreciated,
maintained, and beneficially employed.

Literature Cited

Frankel, O.H. 1970. Variation, the essence of life. Sir
William Macleay Memorial Lecture. Proc. Linn. Soc. 95:
158-169.

Hodgson, R.E., ed. 1961. Germ Plasm Resources. Am. Ass.
Advance. Sci., Washington, D.C., Publ. No. 66. 381 pp.

Schoenewald-Cox, C.M., S.M. Chambers, B. MacBryde, and L.
Thomas, eds. 1983. Genetics and Conservation - A
Reference Manual for Managing Wild Animal and Plant
Populations. The Benjamin/Cummings Publ. Co., Menlo
Park, Calif. 722 pp.

Part 1

History and Policy Development in Agriculture

1. History of Plant Introduction in the United States

Plant introduction is interpreted in various ways. Some individuals apply it to the actual search for plant materials, to be used for specific purposes, and generally, to be grown in an environment which may differ from the original site. Others refer to "introduction" when a newly developed crop variety is being released for public or commercial use. To most crop specialists, however, the term in a broad sense means the transfer of living genetic resources from a location where they usually have survived through many generations to a new location. Regardless of the definition or interpretation, this activity most likely started with man's need for food in early civilizations and has since become the most important factor in his survival.

Historically, an inscription found in Mesopotamia tells of Sargon's crossing the Taurus Mountains to Asia Minor in about 2500 B.C. to bring back tree specimens, vines, figs and roses. The earliest recorded account of an organized plant collecting trip is that of Queen Hatshepsut of Egypt who, in about 1500 B.C., sent ships to the Land of Punt in East Africa to collect the incense tree. It is difficult to trace the introduction of plant germplasm to the New World due to the surge of explorers after Columbus, and the rapid developments associated with commerce and immigration even before the Revolutionary period.

One of the basic reasons for the present status of the U.S. as the world leader in agricultural production lies in the utilization of exotic plant germplasm for crop improvement. Before the colonization period, the North American Indians had access to native food plants such as blueberry, cranberry, pecan, and sunflower as well as corn, beans, tobacco, and cotton naturalized over much of the Americas in general. We might consider the early years of the 19th century as the initiation of our continuing agricultural revolution and the time when plant introduction was recognized as necessary to expanding the full cropping potential of our new land. Similar recognition has occurred in other agriculturally oriented countries, and will continue to be an important factor in the developing countries of today's world. The history of plant introduction in the **United States** might best be reviewed by time periods as follows:

1. Prior to formalized USDA program (1898).
2. Early explorations (1898-1930).
3. Activities before, during and shortly after **World War II** (1930-1948).
4. USDA-States Cooperative Program (1948-1975).

I have based this presentation upon facts provided in various official documents published in recent years, as well as personal experience and background developed as Plant Introduction Officer for USDA since 1948.

Prior to Formalized USDA Program (1898)

Before and after the Revolution, seed and plant materials were brought into the country by immigrants, commercial shippers and traders, government officials, and privately sponsored explorations. A famous quote attributed to Thomas Jefferson in 1790 was, "The greatest service which can be rendered any country is to add a useful plant to its culture." Many individuals involved in these dealings were aware of the crop production and improvement potentials but no organized mechanism existed for distributing, testing, and preserving introductions. The better types were randomly passed or sold from one source to another. Certain family groups maintained seed of a specific good crop from one generation to the next, resulting in what we now refer to as "heirloom" varieties presently being sought by historic farms and gardens. Ben Franklin is credited with setting a precedent for other government officials when during his European visits he sent seeds and plants back to the U.S. A letter from Franklin to Noble Wimberly Jones, October 7, 1772, referred to a shipment of upland rice from Cochin, China and seed of the Chinese tallow tree. President John Quincy Adams provided the first official recognition of such a practice in 1827 when he requested all Consular officials outside the U.S. to forward rare seeds and plants to Washington for distribution.

The problem of distributing early plant introductions was solved, in part, in 1836 when Henry L. Ellsworth,

Commissioner of Patents, took the initiative and started
sending introduced seeds to American farmers, using the
franking privileges of Congressional colleagues. Thus began
informally a congressional seed distribution program which
was to grow eventually to enormous size and was to last
nearly a century (until 1925). In 1839, Congress appropriated $1,000 to aid Ellsworth and his Patent Office in
certain kinds of agricultural activity, including the
handling of introduced seeds. With increasing activity
related to plant introduction came increased federal appro-
priations. In 1847, the first funds were provided for
experimentation with potential new crops, and shortly thereafter studies of sorghum and tea were initiated. Records
from the National Archives, Washington, D.C. show that the
Commissioner of Patents hired Robert Fortune in 1858 to go
to China to collect tea seed. Fortune remained in China
through February 1859 and sent to the United States a number
of ornamental trees and shrubs, as well as plants of
economic significance. Finally, in September 1859, Fortune
produced a detailed document on the culture of the tea plant
in China; this publication became the basis of instructions
for tea culture to potential growers in the South.

In 1862, the USDA was created under President Lincoln's
administration. The importance of plant introduction and
seed distribution was immediately recognized and a Commissioner of Agriculture, Isaac Newton, was appointed. He was
specifically directed "to collect, as he may be able, new
and valuable seeds and plants; to test, by cultivation, the
value of such of them as may require such tests; to propa-
gate such as may be worthy of propagation, and to distribute
them among agriculturists." Agriculture received full
recognition in the government when the first Secretary,
James Wilson, was appointed, and the "Section of Seed and
Plant Introduction" was created in 1898.

Since that time, the USDA unit responsible for coordinating plant introduction and exploration has been known
under the following names for the years indicated.

Section of Seed and Plant Introduction (1898-1903)
Office of Seed and Plant Introduction (1904-1907)
Office of Foreign Seed and Plant Introduction (1908-1925)
Office of Foreign Plant Introduction (1926-1930)
Division of Foreign Plant Introduction (1931-1933)
Division of Plant Exploration and Introduction (1934-1953)
Plant Introduction Section (1954-1957)

New Crops Research Branch (1958-1972)
Germplasm Resources Laboratory (1973-Present)

Early Explorations (1898-1930)

The end of the 19th century found the frontiers of
America's agriculture spreading from border to border, thus
calling for a wide variety of crop germplasm including
tropical crops brought into focus by the Spanish-American
war.   During the first quarter of the 20th century, plant
collecting by direct field exploration was extremely active.
The list of explorers included the names Fairchild, Hansen,
Swingle, Carleton, Rock, Meyer, Cook and numerous others,
each contributing largely to specific crop groups.   David
Fairchild is credited with being the organizer and impetus
behind the Section of Seed and Plant Introduction that
started the U.S. toward its continuous and increasingly
important program of plant exploration and introduction.
The first step was the prepartion and periodic issuance of
Plant Inventories, initiated by Special Agent   O.M. Cook.
(As of January 1976, there exists a historical record of
about 410,000 accessions listed in 182 USDA inventories.)
It might be interesting to note that the first accession
recorded was a cabbage from Russia that had been received by
Professor N.E. Hanson, Agricultural College of South Dakota.
He was responsible, also, for the first recorded collections
of winter hardy fruit germplasm.   The diversity of activity
during the early years can best be explained by the following note recorded in Plant Inventory No. 10 (September 1900
to December 1903.)

"The collections of the several Department agricultural
explorers which are represented in this inventory have also
been gathered from a wide range of the earth's surface.   The
explorations of Dr. S.A. Knapp, the results of which are
represented in the inventory, covered his second voyage to
the Orient in 1901-02, and comprised a trip to Hawaii,
Japan, China, Manila, the Straits Settlements, and British
India in search of information bearing on the rice question
of the South.   Bavaria, Austria, Dalmatia, Greece, Egypt,
Tunis, Algeria and Spain were explored by the writer
(David Fairchild) for brewing barleys, hops, fruits and
forage crops.   Mr. C.S. Scofield made a careful survey of
the leguminous fodder and green manure crops of Algeria and
incidentally a study of the wheat varieties of France.
Mr. M.A. Carleton made a second trip in 1900 through Austria
and Roumainia, into Russia and Central Asia, and returned
through Turkey and Serbia in search of cereals and forage
crops.   Mr. E.R. Lake, a specialist on American prunes, was
sent in 1900 on a short trip to the prune-growing regions of

France.   Dr. J.N. Rose, of the U.S.   National Museum, assisted us in 1901 in his botanizing trips in Mexico to secure a collection of desert plants and varieties of other plants of economic importance.   Mr. Ernest A. Bessey was sent as agricultural explorer on two expeditions in search of hardy alfalfas and more resistant fruits for the North-west.   The first was through Russia to Turkestan in 1902, and the second to the Caucasus in 1903.   Mr. Thomas H. Kearney and Mr. T.H. Means, the latter of the Bureau of Soils, were sent as explorers to the arid regions of Algeria, Tunis, and Egypt in search of better strains of Egyptian cotton and alkali-resistant grains and fodder plants.   Mr. P.H. Rolfs, in charge of the Subtropical Laboratory at Miami, Florida, visited for this Office in 1903, several islands in the West Indies in search of varieties of cassava and other suitable agricultural plants for southern Florida.   Mr. G. Onderdonk, of Nursery, Texas, a specialist on stone fruits, made a trip to Mexico for this Office in search of varieties of this class of fruits for the Southern States."

Frank N. Meyer was perhaps the most renowned explorer, due to the hardships he endured and the germplasm he contributed.   For 13 years (1905-1918) he concentrated collecting in central China, Manchuria, Korea, Siberia, Turkestan and the Caucasus, focusing on fruit, nut and vegetable crops.   The total accessions attributed to his endeavor have not been accurately determined, but fortun-ately, they are on record in the USDA Plant Inventories. During his journeys in China, Meyer collected more than 2,000 species and varieties of plants.   He will be most remembered for his collections of Pyrus calleryana which he could not have envisioned as becoming an outstanding orna-mental.   He also emphasized the beauty and majesty of the white-barked pine, Pinus bungeana, as a tree protected from destruction by the efforts of Buddhist priests who planted them around temples.   A more recent item credited to his work was the release in 1951 of Meyer Zoysia collected in Korea.   The latter is an excellent illustration of the time period often required in determining the full value or potential of introduced germplasm.   Frank Meyer disappeared from a steamer on the Yangtze River June 2, 1918.   After recovery of his body, he was buried in Shanghai.

It became necessary in the early years to provide facilities to test the lesser known crops, followed by quarantine centers to prevent introduction of plant pests. The first such location was the Federal Plant Introduction Garden in Miami, Florida, established in 1898 (the same year

the plant Introduction Service was formalized) and transferred to a new location in 1922 where it remains active
today. Other gardens followed at Chico, California, in 1904;
Savannah, Georgia, in 1919; and Glenn Dale, Maryland, also in
1919. The later facility has been used largely for quarantine propagation of prohibited plant materials.

Time does not permit further detail on specific
materials collected between 1898 and 1930, but it was during
these years that field explorations were at a peak, and
probably contributed more to crop improvement and production
than any other time in our agricultural history. Special
significance is attached to the first large scale introduction of soybean germplasm, received through the 1929-30
explorations of W.F. Morse and P.H. Dorsett. These introductions were ultimately responsible for this crop reaching
such a high level of international importance.

Activities Before, During and Shortly After **World War II** (1930-1948)

The lean years of the early 1930s had a decisive effect
upon plant introduction activities, as well as all other
Departmental programs. Lack of funds and major organizational changes took place prior to the outbreak of W.W.II.
The 1934-35 Westover-Enlow expeditions to Turkestan and
environs contributed immensely to forage crop programs,
particularly alfalfa improvement. Dr. Westover was involved
in several other explorations from 1929 through 1937. It
was also during this period that we became alerted to the
value of domesticated and naturalized plant species to be
utilized by the national programs of the newly created Soil
Conservation Service. Hundreds of collections were brought
together at nursery centers throughout the country for
screening against program objectives. During the actual war
period 1941-1945, practically all plant accessions were
obtained through correspondence or foreign donors.

USDA-States Cooperative Program (1948-1975)

After W.W.II, many significant changes took place in
relation to introduction of germplasm, the most important
being the concept of Regional Plant Introduction Stations
to serve better the interests of federal, state and private
crop specialists. It was recognized, also, that the
collecting, testing and distribution were not only of
national, but also international concern. The world
suddenly became a much smaller place in relation to
communication among crop scientists. International

meetings, technical assistance programs for developing countries, development of international crop centers, training and educational programs for foreign nationals at various U.S. colleges and universities, were all factors leading to increased interest in plant introduction and exchange of germplasm. In 1946, the 80th Congress passed the Research and Marketing Act that included funding for the regional "New Crops" program.

The basic objective was to provide "research to encourage the discovery, introduction and breeding of new and useful agricultural crops, plants and animals, both foreign and native, particularly for those crops and plants which may be adapted to utilization in chemical and manufacturing industries." In order to carry out this directive, four Regional Plant Introduction Stations were established at Ames, Iowa (1947); Geneva, New York (1948); Experiment, Georgia (1949) and Pullman, Washington (1952). Their broad assignment covered introduction, multiplication, preliminary evaluation, distribution and preservation phases, with emphasis directed toward new crops that might be used ultimately as partial replacement of those economic crops considered to be in over-production or surplus. These locations coordinated their activities with the procurement of foreign and domestic crop germplasm directed by the New Crops Research Branch, ARS, Beltsville, Md. The matter of preservation of introduced germplasm was considered highly important. Before the implementation of this cooperative program, approximately 160,000 accessions had been recorded since 1898. It was estimated that only 5 to 10 percent of the accessions could be accounted for in living collections. It was evident that for various reasons we were losing valuable plant assets. Simultaneously with the initiation of the program, efforts were made to establish a National Seed Storage Laboratory with the major responsibility for long term storage and preservation of valuable plant germplasm propagated by seed. This facility became operative in 1958 at Fort Collins, Colorado. Each of the four Regional Stations has similar, but smaller storage facilities for holding working stocks.

In order to carry out the new responsibilities for the Regional Stations, it was necessary to increase exploration activities commensurate with the demands of crop researchers. Their programs resulted in a high degree of sophistication, thus creating more specific demands from available genetic resources. Since 1948, under guidance of the Plant Introduction unit serving ARS, 73 foreign explorations have been completed, involving 45 different collectors. One-quarter of a million accessions have been added to inventory during this period. Emphasis has been placed upon various crop categories which are too detailed to be presented here. Special significance would apply, however, to building up the World Collection of Small Grains, the extensive program for preservation of bean germ-plasm rapidly disappearing in Latin America, the large segment of world sorghums subjected to a conversion program in Puerto Rico, warm season and dryland forage species, drug and medicinal plants, ornamentals and potential new fiber and oilseed crops.

Special mention should be made of the Interregional Plant Introduction Station, Sturgeon Bay, Wisconsin estab-lished in 1949 as part of the 1946 Research and Marketing Act. It has become a national center for potatoes and closely related tuber-bearing species and cooperates with international centers abroad. The station serves as the collection center for such germplasm after proper quarantine clearance. At present there are approximately 4,000 acces-sions in this collection.

We have in the U.S. a rather wide range of environ-ments but, generally, plant introductions with most likely potential have been sought in areas of the world with similar agro-climates. Most of the early explorations concentrated, therefore, in the temperate zones of the Soviet Union, Mainland China and environs. Reference was made earlier to the low percentage of accessions saved, a large proportion of which originated in the above locations. Political conditions prevented exploration or exchanges in the Soviet Union from 1935 to 1959. In 1959, exchanges were initiated with USSR and have reached a profitable level. Four major field explorations have occurred there since 1963 and exchanges are conducted by correspondence. Some degree of a similar program may be anticipated for the People's Republic of China. Encouragement will be given to these programs for obvious reasons.

In our discussion to this point we have omitted refer-ence to the historical and highly important part played by plant quarantine and inspection agencies during the proce-dure of plant introduction. We became more cognizant each day of the importance of preventing entry of plant pests. References to the Hessian fly, Gypsy moth, Japanese beetle, Golden nematode, Mediterranean fruit fly, potato blight, chestnut blight, cereal rusts, and specific fruit viruses illustrate the devastation that may occur from outside sources during some phase of plant exploration and introduc-tion. The first Quarantine Act became effective in 1905, with subsequent changes being made in 1912, 1917, 1926 and 1957 being made to meet specific problems arising from increased flow of plant materials to the U.S. Fortunately, close collaboration has been maintained between the plant introduction headquarters and the presently designated Animal and Plant Health Inspection Service in policing incoming germplasm. This must be a matter of great public concern if we are to ensure the success of our future agricultural program.

In conclusion, I wish to make the point that we have been most fortunate to have a well-documented history of plant introduction activities in the U.S. Other contributors to this volume refer to the urgency in collecting and preserving rapidly disappearing plant genetic resources. The collection and maintenance of these resources by the Plant Introduction Office of the Germplasm Resources Laboratory should continue to make history for future reference.

Bibliography

Creech, J.L. 1962. The Greatest Service. USDA Yearbook of Agriculture. pp. 100-105.

_____ 1974. Highlights of Ornamental Plant Introduction in the United States. The Longwood Program Seminars. Vol. 6. University of Delaware. pp. 20-26.

Hodge, W.H., H.F. Loomis, L.E. Joley and J.L. Creech. April 1956. Federal Plant Introduction Gardens. The national Horitcultural Magazine. Vol. 35, No. 2. pp. 86-106.

_____, and C.O. Erlanson. October-December 1966. Federal Plant Introduction - A Review. Economic Botany, Vol. 10, No. 4. pp. 299-334.

_____, and C.O. Erlanson. 1955. Plant Introduction as a Federal Service to Agriculture. Advances in Agronomy, Vol. 7, Academic Press Inc., New York. pp. 189-211.

Hyland, H.L. 1975. Recent Plant Exploration in the U.S. Crop Genetic Resources for Today and Tomorrow. Vol. 2, Cambridge University Press. pp. 139-146.

Klose, N. 1950. America's Crop Heritage. Iowa State College Press, Ames, Iowa.

Whyte, R.O. 1958. Plant Exploration, Collection and Introduction. FAO Agricultural Studies No. 41. Food and Agriculture Organization - United Nations, Rome.

Some Notes and Reflections upon a letter from Ben Franklin
   to Nobel Wimberly Jones.   October 7, 1772.   Privately
   printed by the Ashantilly Press, Darien, Georgia.   1966.

The National Program for Conservation of Crops Germplasm.
   Progress Report on Federal/State Cooperation.   June 1971.
   University Printing Department, University of Georgia,
   Athens, Georgia.

2. Plant Germplasm Policy

Only a few of our crop plants such as sunflowers, cranberries, blueberries, strawberries, pecans, range and forage grasses, and hops are native to this country. Therefore, the great majority of the economically important plants comprising U.S. agricultural production have their origin abroad. Consequently, it has been imperative that the United States devise and practice an effective system for world-wide exploration and introduction as well as preservation of foreign plants. The history and development of this remarkable system is presented in the previous paper by H.L. Hyland. This achievement is all the more impressive recognizing the succession of constraints and hurdles often encountered through combinations of inaccessibility to certain countries and areas from time to time for various reasons, coupled with levels of program support ranging from modest to meager. The successful attainments and continued progress of exploration and introduction activities can be attributed largely to the perseverance of a handful of highly dedicated scientists and administrators.

In the early years of plant exploration and introduction, many stocks were lost as a consequence of inadequate maintenance facilities. Gradually, though slowly, this inadequacy was recognized and partially met, initially by the establishment of a few federal maintenance stations, and later greatly improved through the Research and Marketing Act of 1946. This Act provided for the establishment of Regional and Interregional Plant Introduction Stations cooperatively supported with funds and staff from the federal government and the states.

The network of plant germplasm stations is known as the National Plant Germplasm System. Activities of units within the System are advised on policy matters and coordinated by

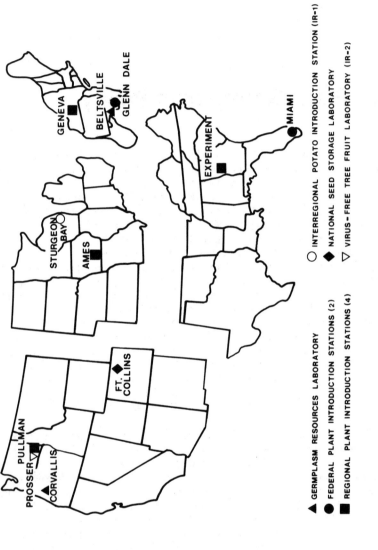

FIGURE 1. Principal stations and laboratories of the U.S. National Plant Germplasm System.

GERMPLASM RESOURCES LABORATORY

▲ FEDERAL PLANT INTRODUCTION STATIONS (2)

■ REGIONAL PLANT INTRODUCTION STATIONS (4)

○ INTERREGIONAL POTATO INTRODUCTION STATION (IR-1)

◆ NATIONAL SEED STORAGE LABORATORY

▽ VIRUS-FREE TREE FRUIT LABORATORY (IR-2)

PULLMAN
PROSSER
CORVALLIS

FT. COLLINS

STURGEON BAY
AMES

GENEVA
BELTSVILLE
GLENN DALE

EXPERIMENT

MIAMI

the National Plant Germplasm Committee. A paper prepared by the Committee entitled "The National Plant Germplasm System" presents the development, present organization and activities of the System.[1] With permission of the Committee, selected portions of this paper are presented.

National Plant Germplasm System

"The National Plant Germplasm System is a coordinated network of institutions, agencies, and research units in the United States which work cooperatively to introduce, maintain, evaluate, catalog and distribute all types of plant germplasm. Primary financial and administrative support for the components of the System comes from the Agricultural Research Service (ARS) of the United States Department of Agriculture and from the State Agricultural Experiment Stations (SAES). Commercial breeding and seed trade interests also contribute to and support the System."

"The elements of the Plant Germplasm System are: (1) the ARS Germplasm Resources Laboratory at Beltsville, Md.; (2) two ARS Plant Introduction Stations at Glenn Dale, Md., and Miami, Florida; (3) four State-Federal Regional Plant Introduction Stations located at Pullman, Wash., Ames, Iowa, Geneva, N.Y., and Experiment, Ga.; (4) the Interregional Potato Introduction Station (IR-1) at Sturgeon Bay, Wis.; (5) the ARS National Seed Storage Laboratory at Ft. Collins, Colo.; and (6) a large group of Federal and State Plant Germplasm Curators located throughout the United States. The Mayaguez Institute for Tropical Agriculture at Mayaguez, P.R. also has responsibility for maintaining some tropical germplasm. In addition, limited germplasm resources are maintained and continuously evaluated by the Interregional Virus-Free Deciduous Tree Fruit Laboratory (IR-2) at Prosser, Wash., and by Regional Project cooperators in the 50 states, Puerto Rico, Guam and the Virgin Islands. The location of the major stations for the National Plant Germplasm System are shown in Figure 1 and Table 1. The cooperating agencies are shown in Table 2."

"Coordination of the research and service functions of these elements is achieved on three sequential levels. Each Agricultural Experiment Station and participating federal agency is represented directly or indirectly on technical committees related to region or interregional stations. Scientsts who serve as technical committee members on these

---

[1]Published as USDA, ARS, Program Aid Number 1188:1-12, 1977.

Table 1. National Plant Germplasm System principal stations or laboratories responsible for introduction maintenance and distribution of plant germplasm

Station or Laboratory	Name and Address	Examples of major collection or regional responsibilities	Remarks
National Seed Storage Lab.	Dr. Louis N. Bass National Seed Storage Lab. Ft. Collins, CO 80521	Gene bank collections of seed crops and their wild relatives	Long-term storage
Germplasm Resources Lab. (Small Grains Cereals Collection)	Dr. Joe C. Craddack Northeastern Region, ARC-West Seed Laboratory Beltsville, MD 20705	World collections of wheat barley, oat, rice and related wild species	National focal point for introduction, documentation, initial distribution, and exchange of plant germplasm. Quarantine and detention nursery; coordination of cereal rust program.
Northeastern Regional P.I. Station	Dr. Desmond D. Dolan N.Y. State Agric. Expt. Sta. Reginal Plant Intro. Sta. Geneva, NY 14456	Perennial clover, onion, pea, spinach, broccoli, timothy	Operating through Regional Research Project NE-9, 12 states. ARS, FS, & SCS participating.
Southern Reginal P.I. Station	Dr. G.R. Lovell Reginal Plant Intro. Station Experiment, GA 30212	Cantaloupe, cowpea, millet, peanut, sorghum, pepper	Operating through Regional Research Project S-9, 14 states. ARS & SCS participating.

Table 1. (cont'd)

Station or Laboratory	Name and Address	Examples of major collection or regional responsibilities	Remarks
North Central Regional P.I. Station	Dr. Willis H. Skrdla Regional Plant Intro. Station Iowa State University Ames, Iowa 50011	Alfalfa, corn, sweet clover, beets, tomato, cucumber	Operating through Regional Research project NC-7, 13 states. ARS & SCS participating
Western Regional P.I. Station Pullman & Central Ferry, Washington	Dr. S.M. Dietz Regional Plant Intro. Station Rm. S9 Johnson Hall Washington State University Pullman, WA 99163	Bean, cabbage, fescue, wheat grasses, lentils, lettuce, safflower	Operating through Regional Research Project W-6, 12 states. ARS, SCS, FS and BLM participating.
Interregional Potato Introduction Lab.	Robert E. Hanneman, Jr. Inter-regional Potato Introduction Station Sturgeon Bay, WI 54235	Solanum tuberosum and Solanum spp.	Operating through Interregional Project 1, SAES and ARS in four regions participating.
ARS Plant Introduction Station	Dr. Howard E. Waterworth Plant Quarantine Facility P.O. Box 88 Glenn Dale, MD 20769	Pome and stone fruits and woody ornamentals	Distributes certified pest-free introductions consisting of prohibited and post-entry quarantine categories of fruits, woody ornamentals and certain vegetables.

Table 1. (cont'd)

Station or Laboratory	Name and Address	Examples of major collection or regional responsibilities	Remarks
ARS Plant Introduction Station	Subtropical Hort. Research Station 13601 Old Cutler Road Miami, FL 33158	Tropical and sub-tropical species including 287 accessions of coffee, 152 mangoes, 160 cacao	
Interregional Virus-Free Deciduous Tree Fruit Lab.	Dr. Paul R. Fridlund Irrigated Agriculture Res. and Extension Center Prosser, WA 99350	Virus-free cultivars of pome and stone fruits	Operating through Interregional Project 2, SAES and ARS in four regions participating.
Northwest Plant Germ-plasm Repository	Otto L. John 33447 Peoria Rd. Oregon State University Corvallis, Ore. 97330	Pears, filberts, small fruits, hops and mints.	

projects not only collaborate in the evaluation of plant introductions but also formally represent the National Plant Germplasm System and provide liaison among other scientists at their respective locations. Some of the representatives of each technical committee are members of the ARS Plant Germplasm Coordinating Committee which is internally advisory to ARS. Several representatives of each technical committee are also members of the National Plant Germplasm Committee (NPGC). The NPGC also includes representation from the national Council of Commercial Plant Breeders and the Cooperative State Research Service."

"These cooperative units, which **constitute** the National Plant Germplasm System, have a general mission of providing plant scientists with the germplasm needed to carry out their research. The research programs that are supported in this way are widely varied and include breeding new cultivars—for resistance to diseases, insects, smog, injury, temperature, moisture, salinity, and other environmental streses; for increased yield and quality; for ease of harvesting, better processing, and longer storage; for beautification, noise abatement, erosion control, and resistance to fire; and as sources of anti-cancer medicinals, analgesics, and industrial chemicals. The well-coordinated operation of the System, under its funding constraints, is evidenced by the reasonably good status of our present plant genetic resources propagated by seed."

"<u>Introduction</u> of plant materials is accomplished through planned foreign and domestic explorations, by exchange with foreign scientists and agencies, and by contributions from travelling scientists. To set up an exploration, breeders, scientists or commodity groups send proposals through the State-Federal regional project structure (see Table 2) for review and possible funding by ARS. The Germplasm Resources Laboratory provided a national focal point and clearinghouse for exchange of plant germplasm with foreign countries. This laboratory also catalogs all incoming accessions, assigns Plant Introduction (P.I.) numbers, makes taxonomic identification, and distributes P.I. material to maintenance centers or other curators according to established regional crop priorities."

"<u>Selected germplasm</u> also enters the National Plant Germplasm System from domestic research programs. These include induced and natural mutations; genetic stocks involving monosomes, trisomes, translocations, marker genes; species hybrids; breeding material with valuable combinations of characters; pest resistant stocks; and

Table 2. Cooperative Input into the National Plant Germplasm System

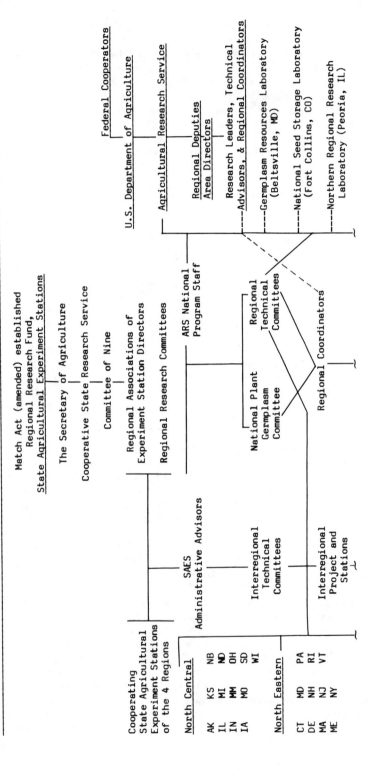

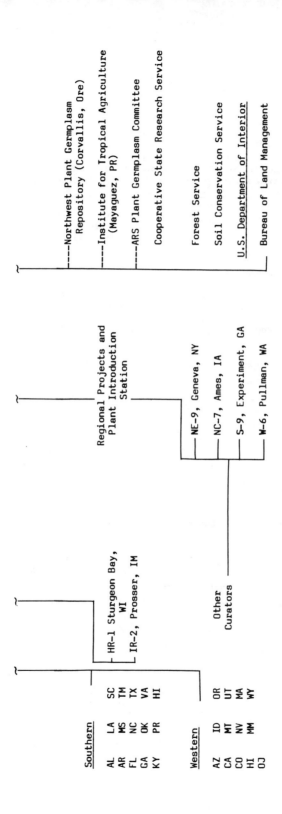

Southern

AL	LA
AR	MS
FL	NC
GA	OK
KY	PR
SC	
TM	
TX	
VA	
HI	

HR-1 Sturgeon Bay, WI
IR-2, Prosser, IM

Western

AZ	ID
CA	MT
CO	NV
HI	MM
OJ	
OR	
UT	
MA	
WY	

Other Curators

Regional Projects and Plant Introduction Station

NE-9, Geneva, NY
NC-7, Ames, IA
S-9, Experiment, GA
W-6, Pullman, WA

Northwest Plant Germplasm Repository (Corvallis, Ore)
Institute for Tropical Agriculture (Mayaguez, PR)
ARS Plant Germplasm Committee

Cooperative State Research Service

Forest Service

Soil Conservation Service

U.S. Department of Interior

Bureau of Land Management

Table 3. Number of plant introductions held and samples distributed by
the various units within the National Plant Germplasm System

Station or Laboratory	Total Plant Introductions held (1975)	Annual Distribution of samples (current)
National Seed Storage Laboratory	90,233	730
Germplasm Resources Laboratory (Small grains collection)	71,870	128,850
North Eastern Regional Plant Introduction Station	20,000	8,998
Southern Regional Plant Introduction Station	28,000	11,981
North Central Regional Plant Introduction Station	20,000	10,500
Western Regional Plant Introduction Station	28,000	28,448
Interregional Potato Introduction Station	4,000	3,400
ARS Plant Introduction Station (Glenn Dale, MD)	9,000	2,775
ARS Plant Introduction Station (Miami, FL)	4,164	3,366
Interregional Virus-Free Tree Fruit Lab.	460	buds 22,520 cultivars 878

obsolete commercial varieties that may have genes useful in the future. Research personnel who develop such material have an obligation to call it to the attention of the appropriate Regional Coordinator or crop curator for inclusion in the maintenance System."

"Maintenance is the responsibility of Regional and Interregional Plant Introduction Stations, curators of collections for specific crops, and the National Seed Storage Laboratory. Curators are individual research scientists with special long-term interests in particular kinds of plant germplasm who agree to maintain plant germplasm in cooperation with Regional and Interregional Stations. The National Seed Storage Laboratory is concerned with the long-term storage of seed. The Regional and Interregional Stations and the germplasm curators must continually replenish plant germplasm by regrowing accessions in the field and greenhouse and preserve viable seed stocks for distribution."

"Evaluation of plant genetic resources is accomplished in several ways: (1) plant introductions are screened initially for a wide range of desirable characteristics, including their resistance to predominant diseases and insects affecting commercial crops to which they are related, and (2) are extensively evaluated in the field, greenhouse and laboratory by cooperating state, federal and private plant scientists for the widely varying traits needed in their research. Results are reported back to the maintenance centers."

"Distribution of plant germplasm is made to all responsible scientists, agencies, and institutions requesting it. All federal and state-federal stations which maintain working collections distributed, free of charge, sufficient quantities of plant material to start their research. The national Seed Storage Laboratory distributes stocks only when material is not available for working collections. Persons who receive plant materials are responsible for acknowledging in publications the source of any material used in their research and for reporting to the supplying agency, the performance of all materials tested."

"Table 3 shows the approximate number of accessions of introduced plants held by the various stations or laboratories and the samples distributed."

"The National Plant Germplasm System is well established and coordinated, and is functioning to fulfill the germplasm needs for minimizing the genetic vulnerability of our major crops. The unmet needs and goals of the System, which have been the subjects of continuing NPGC recommendations for funding, also relate directly to national goals that have been recommended recently by national advisory bodies."

"The National Plant Germplasm Committee coordinates and continually reviews needs of the System. The Committee prepares funding proposals, including proposed funding sources, mechanisms, and amounts, for consideration by SAES, ARS, and other agencies."

"The following more urgent requirements are of high priority:

(a) Establishing repositories for clonally propagated plants such as pome fruits, stone fruits, small fruits, grapes, citrus, nut crops, and subtropical fruits.

(b) 1) Providing for capital improvements, additional staff, and support funds for National, Regional and Interregional Stations and laboratories for the continuing introduction, quarantine, maintenance, distribution, and evalution of plant genetic resources.
2) Establishing, managing, and funding a tropical facility with primary responsibility for increase and maintenance of plant genetic resources.

(c) Funding selected plant germplasm curators throughout the United States.

(d) Identifying the gaps which exist in our major collections and greatly increasing funds for plant explorations designed to fill these gaps.

(e) Computerize, in uniform terms, all plant genetic resource holdings in the United States.

(f) Consolidating our plant genetic resource holdings for safer maintenance at least cost and enhance wider availability to users.

(g) Expanding preliminary evaluation of plant germplasm."

Documentation and Guidelines

A summary of the many and highly significant contributions to science and to improvement of cultivated plants in the U.S. by the germplasm maintained within the

System is documented in the publication "The National Program for Conservation of Crop Germ Plasm" (Anon. 1971). It should be noted in this respect that guidelines for use by state and federal plant breeders utilizing introduced germplasm are presented in "A Statement of Responsibilities and Policies Relating to Development Release and Multiplication of Publicly Developed Varieties of Seed Propagated Crops" (Anon. 1972a). These guidelines outline the procedures involving use of introduced germplasm as related to 1) proper acknowledgment of the originating source 2) prompt publication of research findings and 3) release of improved breeding stocks and cultivars.

The unmet program needs of the National Plant Germplasm System, as previously noted, are several and substantial. These needs, along with a series of additional recommendations directed at 1) strengthening the plant genetic resource base of the United States and 2) maximizing utilization of this base for the improvement of economic plants as well as the advancement of science, are summarized in two highly significant reports:

● "Genetic Vulnerability of Major Crop Plants" (Anon. 1972b)

  and

● "Recommended Actions and Policies for Minimizing Genetic Vulnerability of our Major Crops" (Anon. 1973).

National Plant Genetic Resources Board

One of the recommendations of the latter report has resulted in the establishment of an advisory "National Plant Genetics Resources Board" by the Secretary of Agriculture. The task objectives and duties of the Board as stated in the Secretary of Agriculture's Memorandum No. 1875 of June 3, 1975 are:

"The task of the Board is to advise on the assembly, description, maintenance, and effective utilization of the living resources represented by crop cultivars, primitive, and wild forms of our crops. These resources are vital for plant scientists to have the genetic variability necessary to cope with problems of today and the future."

"The Plant Genetics Resources Board's objectives are to advise the Secretary of Agriculture and officers of the National Association of State Universities and Land Grant Colleges in order to assess national needs and identify high priority programs for conserving and utilizing plant genetic resources including such things as collection, maintenance and description of genetic stocks, and utilization of the stocks in plant improvement programs."

"The duties of the Plant Genetics Resources Board are: (1) to inform themselves of domestic and international activities to minimize genetic vulnerability of crops; (2) to formulate recommended actions and policies on collection, maintenance and utilization of plant genetic resources; (3) to recommend actions to coordinate the plant genetic resources plans of several domestic and international organizations; (4) to recommend policies to strengthen plant quarantine and pest monitoring activities, and (5) to advise on new and innovative approaches to plant improvement."

Conclusion

The past progress and accomplishments of the National Plant Germ Plasm System as measured by the improvement of economic plants through use by state, federal and private scientists of germplasm maintained within the System is impressive. Although it is a costly venture, it has repaid the investment many times over and continues to do so. Further, it is the insurance against unforeseen calamities conditioned by diseases, pests, unfavorable environments or other adverse forces which constantly threaten the abundance of this nation's agricultural production.

But new challenges of overwhelming proportions are ahead. Although modern plant scientists have performed outstanding - indeed sometimes amazing - feats (witness hybrid corn, semi dwarf wheats, IRRI rice, and high lysine corn, to mention a few), the exploding world population demands miracles in food production.

Are plant scientists equal to the task? Their past performances, if one holds to placing bets on winners, favors an affirmative reply to the question.

One vital prerequisite for such a venture is a major and continuing commitment of national resources and effort paralleling that provided human health research in such areas as heart disease and cancer. A solid foundation of genetic resources for building such a program now exists. Further the necessary critical mass of qualified experienced state, federal, and private scientists are available in this country--but the laboratories of most of them suffer from chronic lack of funding by the federal agencies. In other words, accelerated and effective exploitation of this wealth of genetic resources as focused on expanding food needs will require major increases in funding for 1) research, especially basic research, in the plant sciences and 2) training of additional plant scientists. In conclusion, it must be stressed that the time for these increases is now in view of the known considerable lag time between basic science discoveries, their necessary refinement by applied science for translation to modern agricultural technology and their ultimate effective field applications.

Literature Cited

Anon. 1971. National program for conservation of crop germplasm. Univ. Print. Dept., Athens, Georgia. 73 pp.

Anon. 1972a. "A statement of responsibilities and policies relating to development, release and multiplication of publicly developed varieties of seed propagated crops". 9 pages. Exp. Sta. Comm. Organ. and Policy State Univ. and Land Grant Colleges, Agr. Serv. and Soil Cons. Serv., U.S. Dept. of Agr. Mimeo.

Anon. 1972b. Genetic vulnerability of major crop plants. Nat. Acad. Sci., Nat. Res. Council Publ., Washington, D.C. 307 pp.

Anon. 1973. Recommended action and policies for minimizing genetic vulnerability of our major crops. U.S. Dept. Agr. and Nat. Assoc. State Univ. and Land Grant Colleges. 33 pp.

William L. Brown

3. Conservation of Gene Resources in the United States

American agriculture is largely based on introduced germplasm. Had not the early colonists brought with them many of the plant species with which they were familiar in Europe, their diets would have been even more limited than they apparently were. Had they depended solely on plants native to North America, they would have been without bread wheat, other cereal grains, potatoes, and the fruits and vegetables to which they were accustomed. Neither would they have had flax for clothing and linens. They would have had access to sunflowers, some fruits, such as blueberries, cranberries, strawberries, persimmon, wild plum, and to a few species of edible nuts but little else. Consequently, as a nation with a paucity of indigenous crop plants, the U.S. has long been interested in the utilization of introduced gene resources required to meet its growing need for food and fiber.

Current Programs

Gene resource conservation and utilization within the USDA, the State Agricultural Experiment Stations, and the Land Grant Universities received a significant boost with the passage of the Research and Marketing Act of 1946. Under the terms of this Act, federal funds were allotted to states for cooperative research on problems of a regional nature. Among the projects supported by the 1946 Act was one establishing four Regional Plant Introduction Stations (Haugas, 1984) whose primary purpose was to collect, maintain, evaluate, and disseminate germplasm. The four Regional Stations are located at Ames, Iowa; Pullman, Washington; Geneva, New York; and Experiment, Georgia. Each station serves 12-14 states.

The four Regional Plant Introduction Stations and a number of other federal and state supported agencies and institutions **constitute** what has come to be known as the National Plant Germplasm System. These include, (1) The Germplasm Resources Laboratory at Beltsville, Maryland; (2) ARS Plant Introduction Stations at Glenn Dale, Maryland; and Miami, Florida; (3) the Interregional Potato Introduction Station at Sturgeon Bay, Wisconsin; (4) the National Seed Storage Laboratory at Fort Collins, Colorado; (5) the Mayaguez Institute for Tropical Agriculture at Mayaguez, Puerto Rico; and (6) the recently established Clonal Plant Germplasm Repositories at Corvallis, Oregon and Davis, C A. The latter institutions will collect, maintain, and disseminate small fruits, nuts, and other clonally propagated crops.

The Germplasm Resources Laboratory functions as the primary U.S. clearing house for the international exchange of germplasm. The Laboratory receives all incoming accessions, assigns Plant Introduction numbers, makes taxonomic identification, and distributes new accessions to the Regional Plant Introduction stations or other gene banks for maintenance. Additionally, the Laboratory currently maintains the USDA world collection of small grains consisting of wheat, oats, barley, triticale, rye, and rice.

The Interregional Potato Introduction Station, established in 1949, collects, evaluates, maintains, and distributes both wild and cultivated tuber bearing Solanum species. It is the primary U.S. source of potato germplasm for the breeder and potato geneticist.

In 1956, the Congress appropriated $450,000 for the construction of a National Seed Storage Laboratory. At the same time, $100,000 per year was allocated to operational costs. Located at Fort Collins, Colorado, the facility consists of 10 temperature and humidity controlled storage rooms with a combined capacity of 180,000 pint cans. The facility also includes minimal laboratory and office space. NSSL is charged with the long term storage of germplasm in the form of seeds and with the execution of a research program on methods of seed preservation. The laboratory distributes germplasm to users only if requested materials are unavailable from other sources. It is responsible for the maintenance in viable condition of all accessions included in the inventory. The present inventory of the NSSL consists of 116,000 accessions.

The Glenn **Dale,** Maryland facility serves primarily as a quarantine station for vegetatively propagated plant materials. It is equipped to isolate, maintain, and distribute disease free segments of viral and other disease infected introductions.

The Savannah station formerly maintained the principal U.S. bamboo collection and worked also with selection and introduction of new crops but has now been closed.

Tropical and sub-tropical horticultural crops (primarily ornamentals) are maintained by the Miami, Florida Station.

Discussion

The National Plant Germplasm System has provided and continues to provide an essential service to agriculture. Yet, it is fair to say that funding for the system is and has always been inadequate relative to needs. The System operates under the umbrella of a National Plant Germplasm Committee consisting of federal, state, and industry representatives. The Committee provides input relative to policy, the identification of needs and budgetary support for the total system. It is important to note, however, that the Committee serves in an advisory capacity only and, as such, possesses limited decision making authority.

The Committee has identified the following gene resource activities as meriting additional immediate attention.

1. Funding to implement plans for an orderly, phased development of additional clonal repositories.

2. Establishment of a tropical station to provide facilities for research on tropical species and to include a winter nursery where a second generation of materials for increase can be grown annually.

3. Funding of selected curators. The many individuals who maintain gene resource materials frequently do so with funds derived from their research budgets. In an era of declining research budgets, these curatorial activities are usually the first to suffer, and without additional funding, much of the germplasm now in the hands of individual curators could be permanently lost.

4. Identification of gaps in major collections. Most collections are incomplete and, in many instances, the uncollected land races and primitive varieties are being replaced by improved cultivars. It is urgent, therefore,

that those still available be salvaged while it is possible to do so.

5.   Completion of a computerized system for collecting, storing, and retrieving data relative to the National Plant Geneplasm System.

It was not until 1969-70, when Southern Corn Leaf Blight, <u>Helminthosporium</u> <u>maydis</u>, race T., reduced the total U.S. corn crop by an estimated 15 percent, that the nation was awakened to the importance of gene resources and to the potential seriousness of genetic vulnerability.   In 1971, the National Research Council of the National Academy of Sciences appointed a committee to examine the Nation's major crop species with respect to their potential vulnerability to disease and insect pests and to recommend ways to avoid the re-occurrence of crop losses similar to that experienced in maize in 1969-70.   The committee found that many of our important crops rest on a relatively narrow genetic base and, consequently, are genetically vulnerable (NAS 1972).

The basic questions raised in the NRC report were addressed by a sub-committee of the Agricultural Research Policy Advisory Committee (ARPAC) which was organized in 1973 to recommend action and policies relative to the more effective conservation and utilization of plant gene resources (ARPAC 1973).   Among the recommendations of the ARPAC sub-committee was that the Secretary of Agriculture appoint a National Plant Genetics Resource Board (NPGRB) to assure that proper attention and management be given to germplasm resources.   The NPGRB was appointed by Secretary Butz in 1975 and reappointed by Secretary Bergland in 1978.

In the years in which the Board has functioned, it has had a positive influence on federal support for programs in the area of germplasm resource management.   It is also effective in keeping the Secretary informed on the role and importance of germplasm resources in relation to the total agricultural research effort.   The Board's report of March 1979 (National Plant Genetics Resources Board 1979) sets forth in detail a seven-phase program involving federal, state, and private cooperation covering most aspects of research and development relative to the conservation and use of plant genetic resources.   If the recommended program were implemented in its entirety, it would greatly strengthen the National Plant Germplasm System and would go a long way toward meeting current and future needs for gene conservation and management in the U.S.A.

A less tangible but equally important development in recent years has been a growing awareness on the part of society that the germplasm of economic species is an important national resource and its conservation and utilization is equally if not more important than the preservation of endangered species of unknown economic value. Furthermore, numerous institutions and organizations, which in the past have demonstrated little interest in gene resources, are now looking to ways in which they may contribute to solutions to problems associated with germplasm conservation.

Most of the organized effort in germplasm conservation just described has dealt with cultivated plants, forest species, and their wild and primitive relatives. In addition to these activities, a number of programs designed to preserve genetic stocks have been functioning for many years. Among those are the Maize Genetics Cooperation Stock Center currently supported by SEA-AR of the USDA and located at the University of Illinois; a National Soybean Stock Center also located at the University of Illinois; the National Drosphila Species Resources Center at the University of Texas supported by National Science Foundation grants; and the Jackson Laboratory of Bar Harbor, Maine, which maintains uniform genetic stocks of laboratory mice and rabbits.

Animal Germplasm

In contrast to the programs currently in place for the conservation of plant genetic resources, there are no comparable programs for domesticated animals. At present, there seems to be no coordinated effort to preserve existing breeds and strains of any of our domestic animals. Breeders, both public and private, maintain reasonably adequate numbers of breeding stocks of breeds of those species with which they are working during any given period of time. When older breeds are replaced by newer and, presumably, more efficient ones, little attention is given to the preservation of the former. For example, Bereskin (1976) points out that the Galloway breed of beef cattle is in serious danger of extinction since only 19 head were registered in 1975. The same author cites serious declines in the numbers of Dutch Belted dairy cattle, Hereford hogs, Lincoln sheep, and Percheron and Belgian draft horses. In addition to Lincoln, there are three breeds of sheep, Karakul, Old Type Navajo, and Southern Native, nearing extinction in the U.S. (NAS 1978).

Unfortunately, these examples cited for the U.S.A. are

not unique. Rendel (1975) reports that, of the total number of breeds of cattle which existed in Europe and the Mediterranean basin in 1970, only 30 were holding their own and 115 were threatened by extinction.

Among poultry, numerous strains have been lost or are close to extinction because of the almost exclusive use of the White Leghorn breed by the relatively few remaining breeders of white egg layers.

An interesting approach in the conservation of swine germplasm was initiated by Dr. Lavon Sumption at the University of Nebraska in 1958 (Zimmerman and Cunningham 1975). Instead of maintaining separate breeds, a gene pool was developed which included 14 different American and European breeds. The scheme offers a less expensive way of conserving at least some of the genes from a wide range of swine germplasm. Following final incorporation of the 14 breeds, the population was separated into two lines which were subsequently used as base material for a number of selection experiments. This scheme or some modification thereof may be the only practical means of conserving larger animal germplasm until methods are developed for success-fully preserving frozen semen, ova or embryos of most animal species.

One of the reasons for the significant loss of domestic animal germplasm is economic. To maintain animals, particu-larly large animals, in sufficient number to retain the genetic variability characterizing the breed appears at first glance to be an enormously expensive undertaking. Yet the critical question is, how do these costs compare with the potential cost of losing forever genes and gene complexes the future need for which cannot be predicted? Germplasm upon which the nation depends as a food source represents a most important natural resource. Can society afford the continual loss of any significant segment of those resources without seriously jeopardizing its future?

If the nation is really concerned about the conse-quences of the loss of its animal germplasm, and if the costs of maintaining adequate populations of animals is thought to be prohibitive, one logical response to that concern might well be the mounting of a national research program of sufficient size and duration to solve the problems associated with cyrobiological preservation. There are no good biological reasons to assume that, given adequate support, research could not develop techniques of cyrobiological preservation that would permit germplasm conservation in most animals to the degree now possible in dairy and beef cattle through the use of deep frozen semen.

The question is sometimes asked as to why it is neces- sary or even desirable to save older breeds and strains of livestock and poultry if, indeed, modern breeds represent the most efficient genotypes available. While this may be a valid question, there are equally valid arguments to the contrary. As agriculture becomes more sophisticated, the economic value of specific heritable traits tends to change. For example, as more livestock are produced in confinement, those genes which code for response to stress conditions become more important in selection programs; and there is no way of knowing how many such genes may be lost with the disappearance of older breeds. Rendel (1975) refers to the improvement in growth rate in broiler poultry by crossing the Cornish breed with other broiler types. Prior to 1940 the Cornish was an obscure, neglected breed whose usefulness was unsuspected by broiler breeders. Today it is an impor- tant component of most commercial broilers.

In contrast to the almost exclusive concentration on pure line breeding in years past, animal breeders today are placing more emphasis on the exploitation of heterosis in breed and strain crosses. As this practice grows, many of the old breeds may be found to be valuable sources of fitness and other traits in cross breeding programs. To allow those sources of germplasm which may have value in achieving a maximum heterotic response in crosses to disap- pear would be tragic. Nonetheless, this is precisely what has happened and will continue to happen in the absence of an enlightened national program for animal germplasm conser- vation.

Microorganisms

Partly because of the relative ease of maintenance of microorganisms the current status of microbial germplasm conservation is probably better than that of higher plants and animals. Yet within this group of organisms, collec- tions are widely scattered; and some appear not to be readily available (NAS 1978). Microorganisms are maintained by numerous groups including the fermentation and pharma- ceutical industries, university and federal research labor- atories, medical research laboratories, etc., in which main- tenance is primarily to serve in-house needs. With the exception of the American Type Culture Collection, there is no single coordinated agency responsible for the conservation of microbial gene resources. The American Type Culture Collection was organized in 1925 as a private non-profit organization, (ATCC 1979). It maintains some 25,000 collections including bacteria, bacteriophages, fungi, protozoa, algae, and some animal cell cultures. It distributes, on a fee basis, an average of more than 25,000 cultures per year. With increased support, it could perhaps be expanded to serve as a national center for the conservation and maintenance of microbial germplasm. Yet, as has been pointed out by the NRC Committee on Germplasm Resources (NAS 1978), it will probably be impossible to bring together in one location the curatorial expertise needed to manage the large number of types of organisms that should be preserved and made available when needed. The NRC report summarizes the national and international efforts that have been made to compile lists of organizations maintaining microorganisms as well as lists of cultures contained therein. The report clearly points up the need for a greatly expanded and coordinated effort if a reasonably adequate microbial conservation program is ever to be realized.

Current and Future Needs

During the past 45 years, the average per acre yields of major U.S. crops have increased from 33 percent (snap beans) to more than 400 percent (processing tomatoes). Corn yields have increased by 320 percent and wheat by 115 percent. Probably one half of these percentage increases are attributable to breeding and genetics. With this record of success, it is easy to become complacent and to overlook the potential hazards associated with the continually decreasing gene base which undergirds most crop species. Simply stated, genetic vulnerability becomes a subject of concern only when a particular crop is threatened by a new pathogen or insect or becomes susceptible to other stresses imposed by the environment. Harlan (1984) succinctly described the prevailing attitude with respect to the need for implementation of a national plan for germplasm assembly and management when he stated "someone must be hurt before any action is taken."

The nature of the most effective plant breeding program is such that genetic diversity within commercial cultivars of most crop species is gradually being reduced. The breeder, in order to be most efficient and effective, uses primarily as source material for new cultivars the most elite lines, varieties, and strains found within his breeding pool. Segregants from crosses of such materials represent the primary source of new lines, varieties, etc. Inherent within the program, therefore, is the tendency to continually decrease the genetic variability of the breeding pool.

The significant contributions of this breeding effort to increased productivity must be recognized. Despite its success, a serious weakness of the system, however, is its tendency to increase genetic relationships within maturity groups and, consequently, to reduce genetic diversity. If breeding schemes of this nature become so rigid as to exclude the introduction of new and genetically different exotic sources of germplasm into breeding populations, the ultimate result is increased genetic vulnerability. Yet, the use of exotic sources in breeding is fraught with problems. The first obstacle faced by the breeder interested in working with such materials is that of selecting among the thousands of accessions available those few which offer the greatest likelihood of providing the genes or traits required to enhance the value of elite population. This choice would be difficult even if most accessions were accompanied by reliable evaluation data. It becomes almost impossible in the absence of such data. And, with few outstanding exceptions, the absence of evaluation data is the situation most frequently encountered in germplasm collections. Until the accessions are evaluated, documented, and the resulting information made available, it is unlikely that much of the germplasm now residing in the gene banks will be used by the breeder. Without utilization, the gene bank accessions become museum collections the value of which remains unknown.

To rectify this situation will require a costly and long term program of testing and evaluation but if the germplasm now available is to be used, evaluation must be done in order to provide the user with at least minimal data on those attributes of interest. The question is, "Who will do it?"

In my view this is a responsibility of the National Plant Germplasm System. For several species the collection of indigenous land race and wild and weedy relatives is essentially complete. Much effort and considerable resources have gone into collecting, storing, and maintaining these materials. It would be tragic to lose this investment because of a failure to complete the second phase of germplasm management--that of evaluation.

If this need is to be met by the National Plant Germplasm System, it will likely require a restructuring and reorganization of that system. At the very least, it will require a significant increase in budgetary support for the total germplasm management effort. As suggested in a recent report by the General Accounting Office (GAO 1981), it will probably also require a more centralized management of germplasm resources within the National Plant Germplasm System.

Summary

1.   U.S. programs in gene resource conservation have increased markedly since 1970, yet the total effort is still inadequate to meet current needs.

2.   Additional financial support of the National Plant Germplasm System and implementation of recommendations by the National Germplasm Resources Board would go a long way toward meeting current and future needs of gene resource management of higher plants.

3.   Current U.S. programs for animal germplasm conservation are totally inadequate.

4.   The conservation of microbial gene resources could be improved though better organization and collaboration between the various agencies now involved in these activities.

5.   With respect to gene resource management of higher plants, the critical need is in the area of evaluation and documentation. It is suggested that these functions are a responsibility of the National Plant Germplasm System. To be effective, the System will require a significant increase in budgetary support, as well as restructuring, resulting in more centralized management.

Literature Cited

Agricultural Research Policy Advisory Committee.   1973. Recommended actions and policies for minimizing the genetic vulnerability of our major crops.   USDA and national Association of State Universities and Land Grant Colleges, Washington, D.C.   33 pp.

ARS.   1977.   The national plant germplasm system.   Program Aid 1188.   Agricultural Research Service, U.S. Department of Agriculture.   12 pp.

ATCC.   1979.   American Type Culture Collection, Ann. Report 1978.   Rockville, MD.

Bereskin, B.   1976.   Preservation of germplasm--an overview.

U.S. Department of Agriculture, ARS.   Beltsville, MD. 13 pp. mimeo.

GAO.   1981.   U.S. General Accounting Office Report to the Congress. The Department of Agriculture can minimize the risk of potential crop failures.   Gaithersburg, MD. 35 pp.

Harlan, Jack R.   1984.   Gene centers and gene utilization. (This volume).

Haugas, R.W.   1984.   Plant germplasm policy.   (This volume).

NAS.   1972.   Genetic vulnerability of major crops.   National Academy of Sciences, Washington, D.C.   307 pp.

_____.   1978.   Conservation of germplasm resources.   An imperative.   National Academy of Sciences, Washington, D.C.   118 pp.

National Plant Genetics Resources Board.   1979.   Plant genetic resources, conservation and use.   U.S. Department of Agriculture, Washington, D.C.   20 pp.

Rendel, J.   1975.   The utilization and conservation of the world's animal genetic resources.   Agriculture and Environment 2: 101-119.

Zimmerman, D.R. and P.J. Cunningham.   1975.   Selection for ovulation rate in swine: population procedures and ovulation response. Four. Animal Science 40: 61-69.

4. The Canadian Plant Gene Resources Program

Very few of the important agricultural crops grown in Canada are native to the country. Most of them originated as introductions from Europe or Asia. This situation may have arisen from a low agricultural potential in plants of Canadian origin but more probably it may have resulted also from a lack of knowledge, appreciation or interest. It is a well known fact that where Canadian species have been studied intensively, the results have been good and justify clearly further exploration among native and naturalized species. In general, however, the genetic vulnerability of this material has not been great and consequently it has not created problems in connection with the preservation of native and naturalized species. Nevertheless, certain varieties and sources of early corn and alfalfa represent important examples of genetic material in imminent danger of extinction. The encroachment of urban and industry construction in geographically restricted areas, e.g., the Niagara peninsula or the lower Fraser Valley; changes in ecological sites, e.g., flooding caused by hydro developments; alterations in flora resulting from extensive forest harvesting operations or strip mining in certain areas; as well as other activities of man all intensify the risk of complete loss or drastic reduction of natural populations.

While the Canadian situation is not as serious as that in many countries, it might take on much larger proportions in the future if no concerted effort were made to preserve the plant genetic resources - the plant germplasm - of the country. As new varieties replace old ones, Canada must ensure that the pool of genes carried by the obsolete varieties is not lost forever because many of these genes influence characters that may be needed in future plant breeding programs. Among these would be insect resistance, tolerance to disease, winter hardiness, specific morphological characteristics, and ability to withstand a wide range of environmental conditions. They represent an extremely valuable source of genetic material for future use by the plant breeder.

The Formal Recognition of the Importance of Plant Gene Resources in Canada

It was at a national work planning meeting[1] of interested individuals in 1968 that the importance of plant gene resources was formally recognized in Canada. Participants at the meeting included representatives of federal and provincial governments, universities, interested scientific societies (Canadian Society of Agronomy, Canadian Society for Horticultural Science, Genetics Society of Canada), the Canadian International Biological Program, and other concerned individuals. One of the recommendations from that meeting was that Canada should develop a national policy on the maintenance of germplasm arising from sources such as working collections, breeding programs, land races and primitive cultivars existing across the country and further, that this policy also provide for the preservation of these resources in seed banks, nurseries or by other means. Other recommendations were that Canada should develop or adopt a standardized computer system for the recording, storage and retrieval of information on sources and collections of germplasm, and that Canada expand its programs related to plant exploration and to national and international exchanges of plant germplasm.

As a result of these recommendations, the Research Branch of Agriculture Canada established a Central Office devoted to Plant Gene Resources in the fall of 1970 with a full-time Gene Resources Officer. The following year a national Canada Committee on Plant Gene Resources (now known as the Expert Committee on Plant Gene Resources) was established as an advisory body with representation from different provinces, the federal Department of Agriculture and three Canadian scientific societies in Horticulture, Agronomy and Genetics. The committee meets annually, usually in November.

The Objectives of the Plant Gene Resources Program

The objectives of the Plant Gene Resources program have broadened steadily since its establishment in 1970. At

---

[1]Summary report and recommendations. Work planning meeting on plant gene resources of Canada, Ottawa, March 26-27, 1968. (Unpublished).

present, the program includes the following: 1) the production of catalogues or inventories of the plant gene
resources maintained in individual working collections of
Canadian plant breeders and other plant scientists; 2) the
creation of computerized data banks on crops of economic
importance in Canada; 3) the provision of a 'query service'
to plant breeders and others for locating genetic stocks and
cultivars with certain specific characteristics or a combination of these; 4) the preservation and maintenance of plant
germplasm; 5) the exchange of genetic stocks and cultivars
both at the national and international levels; 6) the
participation, on Canada's behalf, in the program of the
International Board for Plant Genetic Resources to establish
a world network of gene banks for international storage of
valuable germplasm collections; 7) the support of collecting
expeditions to collect foreign and native plant material; 8)
the establishment of grant-supported research on plant
genetic resources at universities and other research insti-
tutes; 9) the provision of a focus for Canadian activities
in plant gene resources; and 10) the publication of a newsletter (PGRC Newsletter[1]) to report gene activities in
Canada and elsewhere.

Inventory of Plant Gene Resources

A 1971 survey of plant breeders in the country established a national record of the extent and location of
genetic stocks maintained in individual working collections. Some 86,000 stocks were identified as being held by
167 plant breeders. These represent genetic stocks, old and
new varieties, breeding lines and wild relatives of crops
grown in Canada. For example, the number of stocks reported
for barley was 6,000; for wheat 9,000; for oats, 13,000; and
for corn, 3,000. A total of 81 genera are represented in
the collections. Table 1 shows the number of stocks in
working collections of plant breeders for a selected group
of crops.

The first task of the Plant Gene Resources Office was
to develop a system of orderly recording of genetic stocks
and other gene resources of barley, tomato, alfalfa, wheat
and oats maintained in the working collections of Canadian
breeders. The Office developed computer compatible crop
information forms for each of these crops. A completed form
contains information on between 72 and 84 descriptors,
depending on the crop.

---

[1]Publication of the PGRC Newsletter began in 1976. It is
published semi-annually, and is available from the PGRC
office.

Table 1. Number of genetic stocks maintained in working collections of Canadian plant breeders for a selected group of crops in 1971

Crop plant	Number of collections	Total number of stocks
Alfalfa, Medicago species	18	3,100
Apple, Malus species	8	950
Barley, Hordeum species	20	6,000
Bean, Phaseolus species	3	110
Bentgrass, Agrostis species	3	360
Birdsfoot trefoil, Lotus species	7	1,350
Bluegrass, Poa species	6	1,350
Bromegrass, Bromus species	7	650
Buckwheat, Fagopyrum species	2	225
Corn, Zea mays	10	3,000
Cucumber, Cucumis sativus	3	55
Currant, Ribes species	5	235
Fababean, Vicia faba	2	215
Fescue, Festuca species	5	780
Flax, Linum usitatissimum	4	1,900
Grape, Vitis species	6	300
Oat, Avena species	21	13,000
Orchardgrass, Dactylis glomerata	4	150
Peach, Prunus persica	4	520
Pear, Pyrus communis	8	435
Pepper, Capsicum frutescens	1	100
Potato, Solanum tuberosum	4	1,000
Plum, Prunus domestica	5	440
Raspberry, Rubus idaeus	6	1,200
Reed canarygrass, Phalaris arundinacea	4	250
Rye, Secale cereale	5	300
Soybean, Glycine max	4	1,000
Strawberry, Fragaria x ananassa	6	1,330
Sweetclover, Melilotus species	3	375
Timothy, Phleum pratense	6	400
Tobacco, Nicotiana tabacum	2	50
Tomato, Lycopersicon esculentum	14	10,350
Triticale, Triticale hexaploide	1	200
Wheat, Triticum species	28	9,000
Wheatgrass, Agropyron species	8	1,200
Wild rice, Zizania aquatica	2	45

The documentation aspect of the plant gene resources program is totally dependent on the participation of scientists and is the part of the program that has progressed the least rapidly. Less than 2,200 of an estimated total of 41,450 stocks of barley, tomato, alfalfa, wheat and oats had been identified and described by the end of 1978. The support from scientists at research stations and universities has been less than satisfactory because of other priorities and also because of their limited resources to carry out the necessary work.

The Expert Committee on Plant Gene Resources has now recognized that perhaps it had been too much to expect plant breeders and other plant scientists to provide full descriptions of each of the stocks in their working collections. One reason is that stocks are included in collections generally not because they are superior for all traits but because of only one or two traits for which they are known to be superior. Little information is available to the breeder on other traits in which he is not particularly interested. In other words, a breeder generally knows very few details about the stocks in his working collection except for possibly one or two traits for each stock.

In view of this and to facilitate the participation of plant breeders in its inventory program, the Committee agreed at its 1978 annual meeting to concentrate on the creation of trait inventories instead of the attempted variety inventories. It was recognized however, that the creation of trait inventories would still require the participation of plant breeders but that it called for much less work on their part.

Some progress has been made in developing trait inventories of Canadian genetic resources. In June 1979 more than 150 breeders, pathologists and other plant scientists were contacted and they were asked to provide: 1) list of traits that they considered important for the species they were working with; 2) lists of cultivars, genetic stocks and experimental lines in their individual working collections that best expressed the different traits; and 3) 50-gram seed samples of each stock on their lists for long-term storage at the Plant Gene Resources Office. The number of stocks identified and described is now close to 9,000, but it is still far from the total number of 86,000 stocks reportedly being maintained in individual working collections.

In a 1980 review of the plant gene resources program, more particularly its documentation aspect, it was recommended that assistance be provided to scientists to sort out and describe valuable germplasm for inclusion in the crop data banks. It was suggested that this might be achieved by use of Summer Corps (students) or similar work programs at stations and universities where crop breeding programs are located. Another recommendation was to give higher priority and greater recognition to the description and preservation of genetic stocks as an essential phase of plant breeding.

Crop Information Banks

The Plant Gene Resources Office has, to date, created data banks for the barley, tomato, alfalfa, wheat and oat crops. Plans have been made to create data banks for corn, sunflower, peas, apple and tobacco in the coming year. An IBM version of TAXIR, an information storage and retrieval system, is used in the creation of these crop information banks.

Inventories (Loiselle 1980a,b,c) of Canadian barley, tomato and wheat genetic resources were published in 1980 by the Plant Gene Resources Office. They are computer-produced lists of cultivars and genetic stocks from working collections of plant breeders classified under various important traits specific to each crop. As mentioned previously, the trait inventories, as opposed to the variety inventories attempted earlier, were started in 1979 in an effort to promote a greater response from plant breeders in the inventory aspect of the Canadian program on plant gene resources.

The usefulness of such crop information banks and of the crop inventories will increase as the information about each stock becomes more complete and as the number of stocks in the inventories gets larger.

Seed Preservation at the Plant Gene Resources Office

Long-term and medium-term seed storage facilities are available at the Plant Gene Resources Office to preserve the seeds of plant gene resources available in the country. In addition they are used to store international base collections of Pennisetum millet and oats as Canada's participation in the program of the International Board for Plant Genetic Resources to establish a world network of gene banks for cooperative genetic preservation.

Stocks presently preserved at the Plant Gene Resources Office total approximately 60,350. Table 2 lists the

various collections together with the number of stocks in
each.

Table 2.   Stocks preserved as seed at the Plant Gene
Resources Office in 1980

Collection	Number of stocks
CAV Collection (oats)	5,900
CHC Collection (barley)	2,600
CN Collection (alfalfa, barley, oat, tomato, wheat)	4,000
PGR Collection (introductions, various crops)	10,000
IBPGR International Millet Collection	600
California Wheat Collection	1,250
Regina Wheat Collection	3,500
USDA World Barley Collection	16,000
USDA World Flax Collection	3,000
USDA World Oat Collection	12,600
Miscellaneous stocks	500
Total	60,350

Facilities for seed preservation include: 1) 54 cubic
metres of medium-term storage with temperature (+4°C) and
humidity (20%) control and using open storage, i.e., seed
stored in paper envelopes; 2) 64 cubic metres for long-term
storage with temperatures at -20°C and no humidity control
and using sealed storage, i.e., seed stored in sealed
containers (laminated paper/foil/polyethylene envelopes[1]).
An additional 81 cubic metres for long-term storage is being
added.   As more seed storage facilities are provided, the
Plant Gene Resources Office should be in a better position
to serve as a reservoir for other plant collections such as
the European-Canadian rapeseed collection being established
in Braunschweig, Federal Republic of Germany, with a dupli-
cate to be stored at Ottawa.

Clonal Repositories for Tree Fruit Germplasm

The preservation and maintenance of tree fruit germplasm involves a procedure much more complex than for
genetic material that can be stored at low temperature as
seed.   Because fruit trees are propagated vegetatively,

---

[1]Available from Disbrow Envelope Corporation, Jersey City,
New Jersey, 07305, U.S.A.

clones must be maintained in a growing condition and thus require land and reasonable attention and care.

Clonal repositories for the preservation of tree fruit germplasm are being established at six Agriculture Canada Research Stations (Kentville, St-Jean, Harrow, Morden, Summerland, Sidney) and at the horticultural Research Institute of Ontario at Vineland. As participants in the clonal repositories program, the directors of each institution have agreed: 1) to not eliminate any of the 'heritage' cultivars that are presently growing on their station without notifying the Plant Gene Resources Committee far enough in advance to permit propagation at another suitable location (about two years) and 2) to set aside a suitable location at their station for a clonal repository that will permit the maintenance of a moderate number of clones (30-60) of designated specific cultivars and genetic stocks.

Two types of fruit material have been identified by the Committee as important for preservation: 1) specific gene sources, e.g., the compact gene in apples or sources of apple scab resistance; and 2) heritage cultivars, including many old varieties, some of them distinctly Canadian, that include unique combinations of characters and are not grown commercially at the present time. The Gene Resources Committee of the Canadian Society for Horticultural Science is finalizing the lists of apple cultivars to be preserved. Two hundred and fourteen apple stocks have been tentatively included in these.

Cryopreservation of Plant Genetic Resources

The possibility of utilizing tissue cultures and freeze storage for the preservation of important and rare genetic resources, especially of vegetatively propagated plants, is being considered by the Expert Committee on Plant Gene Resources. Dr. Kutty Kartha (Kartha et al. 1979) and his colleagues at the NRC's Prairie Regional Laboratory in Saskatoon are working on a research program to make freeze preservation of living plants a practical proposition. Working with field peas, they have developed a method of freezing pea meristem cells at $-196^{\circ}C$, the temperature of liquid nitrogen. At this point, almost all biological activity is at a standstill and the cells exist in a kind of "suspended animation" little affected by the passage of time. The precise method of protecting each plant species against freeze damage in cooling and thawing will have to be determined through research.

The application of freeze storage and tissue culture to the preservation of apple will be investigated to determine their practicality in the long-term preservation of important apple genetic resources and to establish the precise technology required. A contract program to support such research at a university should be in operation in 1981.

Collecting Expeditions

Agriculture Canada in the past 15 years has sponsored some seven foreign collecting expeditions, which resulted, among others, in the world's most comprehensive wild oat (Baum et al. 1975) and barley collections. Exploration and collection of native plant material have resulted in collections of forage species of northern grasses from Alberta and the Northwest Territories, collections of strawberry clones from the coast of British Columbia and collections of the North American red raspberry from British Columbia. Universities have also collected native plant material. It has been proposed that collection of native germplasm, taxonomic and ecological research and the development of centers of excellence for specific genera or plant groups be supported at universities through the use of the federal grant-supported research program.

National and International Exchanges of Genetic Resources

National as well as international exchanges of plant genetic material and also of information represent another important activity of the Canadian program. The Plant Gene Resources Office is widely recognized as a seed exchange center at both the national and international levels. In the period 1971-1980 it exchanged almost 60,000 stocks. In 1980 alone, a total of close to 275 exchanges with 37 countries for 9,500 stocks were completed. Almost 10,000 accessions have been introduced by the Office since 1971.

Conclusions

The Canadian plant gene resources program is now well established. Its initial objectives as defined in 1970 were concerned only with the documentation and classification of our native grass species; the cataloguing of our plant breeding material; the provision of support for the collection of plant breeding material from around the world; and, the formation of a committee plant gene experts. The objectives have increased steadily in the past 10 years and new ones include, among others, the creation of computerized data banks on crops of economic importance in the country and the provision of a "query service" to plant breeders for locating genetic stocks with certain specific traits; the preservation and maintenance of plant germplasm; the exchange of genetic stocks and cultivars at both the national and international levels; the participation in the program of the International Board for Plant Genetic Resources for international storage of valuable germplasm collections; the establishment of grant-supported research on plant genetic resources at universities; and the publication of a newsletter to report on plant gene activities in Canada and in other countries.

Literature Cited

Baum, B.R., T. Rajhathy, J.W. Martens, H. Thomas.   1975. Wild oat gene pool, a collection maintained by the Canada Department of Agriculture.   Research Branch, Canada Department of Agriculture, Publication 1475 (revised), 100 pp.

Kartha, K.K., N.L. Leung, O.L. Gamborg.   1979.   Plant Science Letter 15: 7-15.

Loiselle, R.   1980a.   Canadian Barley Genetics Resources Inventory/Inventaire canadien des ressources génétiques de l'orge.   Central Office for the Plant Gene Resources of Canada, Ottawa Research Station, Research Branch, Agriculture Canada, PGRC-80-1, 206 pp.

Loiselle, R.   1980b.   Canadian Tomato Genetic Resources Inventory/Inventaire canadien des ressources génétiques de la tomate.   Central Office for the Plant Gene Resources of Canada, Ottawa Research Station, Research Branch, Agriculture Canada, PGRC-80-2, 264 pp.

Loiselle. R.   1980c.   Canadain Wheat Genetic Resources Inventory/Inventaire canadien des ressources génétiques du blé.   Central Office for the Plant Gene Resources of Canada, Ottawa Research Station, Research Branch, Agriculture Canada, PGRC-80-3, 142 pp.

Part 2

Genetic Resources in Forest and Wildlife Management

5. The California Gene Resource Conservation Program

<u>The California Program</u>

The California Gene Resource Conservation Program was initiated in September 1980 by the state of California. It is a 24-month program, funded at $770,000, whose major goal is to provide the documentation and assistance needed to ensure that the animal, plant, and microbial gene resources important to California are appropriately safeguarded. Part of this effort is to determine what role the state should have in the management and conservation of the gene resources from which the basic needs of California are derived (e.g., agricultural, forestry, fish, pharmaceuticals, energy, and other products). Another responsibility is to identify specific gene resource-related needs such as new legislation, additional conservation and research activities, changes in policies and programs, and increased support.

The program is a collaborative effort directed and guided by advisory committees comprising members of both the public and private sectors--legislators (Republicans and Democrats), state and federal agencies, the academic community, industry, and conservation organizations. The National Council on Gene Resources, a research and education organization, is conducting the Program. California's program is a model and a catalyst for similar efforts elsewhere.

California has a situation similar to that of other states and countries such as Canada and the United States which have outstanding agricultural, forestry, or fishing industries, all of which are dependent on gene resources. These states and countries stand to reap tremendous economic and other benefits if they can meet increases in worldwide demand predicted for food and fiber (due mostly to the estimated increases in world population size). Taken together, the following factors imply that the development of new plant varieties is likely to increase in importance as a cost-effective and safe method for meeting these future increases in demand for bioresources:

1)   additional production will have to come mainly from increases in productivity (yield/acre) because the projected increases in arable land are much smaller than the estimated increases in demand;

2)   predictions indicate that monocultural practices will increase throughout the world, and that crops and trees will become more vulnerable to losses from insects and disease damage; and

3)   the costs of energy intensive methods to increase productivity and reduce crop and timber losses (such as applying fertilizers and pesticides) are becoming prohibitively expensive.

Reports indicate that to develop new successful varieties current breeding populations need infusions of new genetic diversity found in land races and the wild relatives of current breeding populations.

While California, some other states, and Canada have the potential to acquire similar benefits, they also share many of the same problems. For example, essentially all commercially grown crops and livestock in the U.S. originated or were first domesticated in other countries. This means that the United States and Canada have considerable dependence on crop and livestock gene resources found in other countries, many of them less developed ones. A challenge exists to fill current collections with samples of the remaining uncollected land races, primitive breeds, and wild relatives before they are replaced by a few modern varieties and breeds, or destroyed, for example, through changes in land use practices. In addition, a more difficult task must be undertaken to institute practical measures to safeguard, in situ, wild relatives of domesticated crop and livestock species.

There are similar challenges for California, the United States, and Canada in managing and conserving the gene resources of their vast forests and fisheries. However, because these forests and fisheries are native there is a greater chance to maintain these gene resources, both in situ and ex situ. Collections can be made before harvesting; and harvesting and restocking techniques can be

adjusted to make them consistent with the maintenance, in
situ, of appropriate genetic diversity. Finally, Gene
Resource Management Areas can be established to maintain
appropriate samples of the genetic diversity of individual
populations or species, and the animal and plant communities
of which they are a part.

Genetic Resource Management

The Problem. The 1970's witnessed a rapidly growing
concern in the United States and elsewhere for the status of
the animals, plants, and microorganisms essential to human
existence. Reports such as those of the U.S. National
Academy of Sciences (1972 1978) and the more recent
Global 2000 (U.S. Council on Environmental Quality 1980)
and World Conservation Strategy (I.U.C.N. 1980) indicated
that gene resources are rapidly disappearing through the
destruction or significant alteration of natural habitats,
losses of traditional animal breeds and crop cultivars
through replacement with modern stocks, and poorly maintained or discarded collections. Unfortunately, there is
insufficient financial support and institutional coordination to prevent these losses. Not only are conservation
measures inadequate but research is lagging. For example,
improved methods are needed for accurately predicting the
short and long-term effects of management practices on
genetic diversity. In addition, improved, cost-effective
methods need to be developed for in situ and ex situ conservation for assessing the need for new germplasm, and for
predicting the potential utility of untested germplasm. As
improvements are made in these areas, it is likely that
fewer gene resources will have to be maintained and that
fewer losses will occur. This, in turn, will lower maintenance costs while, at the same time, improving production.

Lack of financial support has contributed to poor coordination among and within the several public agencies and
private organizations concerned with gene resources.
Coordination is necessary because responsibility for
activities affecting gene resources important to California,
the U.S., Canada, and other countries is divided among
federal, state, and international agencies, other countries,
and the private sector. Individual species or commodities
may be affected by different organizations with policies and
programs which differ greatly from one another. For
example, Douglas fir, one of the most commercially valuable
timber species in the U.S., occurs naturally in different
states such as California, Oregon, and Washington; on
federal lands controlled by several federal agencies; and on

private lands regulated by different state agencies. In
addition, a single agency may have more than one program
affecting the same population or species.

Responses to these problems have included those of the
Committee on Germplasm Resources of the U.S. National
Academy of Sciences (National Academy of Sciences 1978)
which called for increased funding for appropriate conservation measures, research, and other related activites. In
addition, the Committee recommended changes in policies and
programs including the formation of a new federal agency(s)
and increased powers for existing ones.

Yet, in spite of the vital importance and the need for
new gene resources, in spite of the serious consequences
resulting from their losses, and furthermore, in spite of
the efforts of individuals and public and private organization, no significant increase in support has been forth-
coming. Gene resource conservation remains a low priority
issue at all levels--state, national, and international.

How can such a situation exist? After all, animal,
plant, and microbial species provide tremendous economic and
social benefits to all individuals and interest
groups--government, industry, conservationists, research
institutions and consumer groups.

Obstacles. Three major obstacles have been identified
that need to be overcome before major progress can be made
in the U.S. (and these probably apply to other countries as
well).

Perhaps the most important obstacle is the fact that
most key decision makers are unaware or have only a partial
understanding of the broad range and seriousness of gene
resource related problems. Most of these persons who have
the power and influence to remedy the current situation
(e.g., the U.S. President, cabinet members, governors,
legislators, and corporate and government executives) have
observed the high productivity of U.S. agrciulture, forestry
and fishing industries. However, few of these responsible
decision makers realize that the continued success of renewable resource based industries depends on the dwindling
reservoirs of irreplaceable gene resources.

The lack of an active, organized, broad base of support
at any level (e.g., national and state) is the second
critical obstacle. The management and conservation of gene
resources important to the U.S. is an ongoing task involving

a broad range of very complex problems. No single individual, organization, or sector can make significant headway.
In fact, failures in the past to attract additional support
and to coordinate policies and programs can be partially
attributed to the fact that most individuals and organizations have acted alone (understandably) in attempts to
remedy only those gene resource conservation problems in
which they have been actively involved. An ongoing,
well-organized broad based effort comprising interested
individuals and representatives of public and private
organizations is essential for long-term progress in
overcoming gene resource problems.

The third obstacle is the lack of documentation that
persons with budget and policy making authority require in
order to justify significant changes in policies and in
funding.

Solutions. Information is needed on hundreds of
species regarding the specific measures required to appropriately manage, conserve, and utilize their gene resources.
Data is needed to answer basic questions such as:

● What conservation measures should be taken? When?
    Where?
● What research should be supported? At what levels?
● What monitoring and surveying should be supported?
● What changes in laws, policies, and programs are the most
    important?
● What are the costs and benefits?

With the above information, coordinated and cost-effective plans can be developed, and with this documentation key
decision makers will be able to provide the active leadership and support required to appropriately safeguard gene
resources.

Recent experience has shown that little overall
progress will result from information concerning only one
species, problem, or technique. For example the 1970 corn
leaf blight in the United States was a key event that
focused considerable attention in the U.S. on its gene
resource related problems. Yet, little substantial improvements have been made to prevent similar problems from occurring and we may not be so fortunate next time in quickly
arriving at acceptable solutions.

The California Gene Resource Conservation Program as
well as national efforts of the National Council on Gene
Resources have been designed with the intention of over-

coming these major obstacles discussed above. Two main approaches are being utilized. The first is to involve key decision makers from both the public and private sectors in all aspects of program activities. This will increase their understanding of gene resource problems and also increase the chances that proposed solutions will be practical, effective, and implemented. The second approach is to provide the type of information that will justify significant changes needed in policies, programs, or funding.

Phase One of the California Program

The first phase of the two-phase California program lasted six months (September 1980 to March 1981). Its main objectives were to provide the background information for policy makers concerning gene resources; to start a gene resources data base; and to develop a standard procedure for assessing the gene resource needs of individual species or commodities (National Council on Gene Resources 1981). The gene resources data base will be regularly up-dated, and will make it possible to develop coordinated and cost-effective gene resource management plans. In gathering data we have found that not only is appropriate information widely-scattered, but much relevant data are not available because they are not collected. For example, a survey in 1980 showed that genetic diversity of plants and animals (domesticated breeds and varieties and wild species) is not monitored on a regular basis. Furthermore, while information regarding the overall production of individual crops is readily available, similar data on individual varieties is not. This makes it difficult to anlyze the costs and benefits regarding the conservation of gene resources in relation to development of new varieties.

The development of standard procedures to assess needs of individual species and to develop coordinated plans will be of tremendous utility. First, it will remove much of the variation in making assessments that are due to differences between the professionals who make them. Second, it will ensure that the absence of information is due, most likely, to its unavailability, and not to any oversight on the part of the assessor. Third, it will be a basic tool for the development of comprehensive plans and assigning priorities on the relative merits of the gene resource needs of different species and commodities.

Phase Two of the California Program

During the second phase of the California program (March 1981 to July 1982) assessments and plans will be developed for managing the gene resources of six key species or commodities of importance to California. Douglas-fir (1) and strawberries (2) are the first ones selected. The other four commodities or species will include: cattle or poultry (3); salmon (4); a fruit or nut tree (5); and a terrestrial game animal such as ducks or deer (6).

Assessments and plans are developed in three stages. First, data are collected so that the following specific needs can be identified and evaluated:

1) the measures required for in situ and ex situ conservation;
2) research;
3) the collection, analysis, and dissemination of data;
4) changes in legislation, policies, and programs; and
5) modifications in levels of support.

Additional information is collected so that the following factors can be utilized to assign priorities during the development of management plans:

1) the relative importance of a species;
2) the need for new genetic diversity, including its urgency;
3) the threats to existing genetic diversity and their magnitude;
4) the chances of accruing benefits from infusions of new genetic diversity; and
5) the benefits and costs of alternative actions.

The second stage is to develop the management plan, and the third stage is to implement it.

Each plan is developed and implemented through a collaborative effort involving representatives of existing interest groups--legislators, state and federal agencies, industry, the academic community, and conservation organizations. The opportunity exists to explore the possibility of a cooperative effort among California, other states, and industries which benefit from the growth, harvesting, processing, or utilization of the gene resources important to California. For example, the state governments of Oregon, Washington, California, and the timber industry might provide support to assess and meet the needs related to Douglas fir's gene resources. These six plans will be models and catalysts for making similar efforts regarding other important species and commodities which need further attention.

The Long Term California Program

There are two additional objectives of the California program: (1) to determine the needs and alternatives for a long-term Gene Resource Conservation Program in California; and (2) to analyze the needs and options for improving research in California regarding the management, conservation, and utilization of gene resources. The following questions will have to be addressed:

- What should California's responsibility be for the gene resources important to the state?
- What ongoing capability should California have, if any, in identifying, addressing, and resolving gene resource related problems?
- What are the most efficient and effective methods for providing this capability?
- What are the best methods for meeting the research needs related to California's gene resource conservation problems?

No business or society that depends on renewable living resources can remain successful without making sufficient capital investments. In this case they are in irreplaceable gene resources. This presents California, the U.S., and other countries with huge and extremely difficult management problems. However, the fact that gene resources are so vital, and that the costs are so small in comparison with the expected benefits, makes these investments all the more worthwhile.

Literature Cited

International Union for the Conservation of Nature and Natural Resources. 1980. World Conservation Strategy. Morges, Switzerland.

National Council on Gene Resources. 1981. California Gene Resource Conservation Program. Phase I Report. Berkeley, California.

U.S. Council on Environmental Quality and the U.S. Department of State. 1980. Global 2000. Washington, D.C.

U.S. National Academy of Sciences. 1972. Genetic Vulnerability of Major Crops. Washington, D.C.

U.S. National Academy of Sciences. 1978. Conservation of Germplasm Resources. Washington, D.C.

6. Native Plant Gene Conservation in British Columbia

History

The formal commencement of the conservation of genetic resources of native plant species began in many countries around the globe with the International Biological Program of the early 1960's. One of the central purposes of this program was to set aside natural areas (I.B.P. Conservation Terrestrial) to protect gene pools. Fosberg (1981) gives an overview of natural area preservation in the world, as do McLaren and Peterson (1975) in Canada, and Krajina (1976) in British Columbia.

In British Columbia, Krajina (1969) laid the basis for the selection of ecological reserves by developing his classification of Biogeoclimatic Zones. He also led the drive to convince the British Columbia Government to pass an Ecological Reserves Act in 1971.

Foresters were involved early in the attempt to set aside natural areas for research. Romancier (1974) recorded the early work on Aldo Leopold and the U.S. Forest Service in the early 1920's. Weetman (1972) outlined the policy of the Canadian Institute of Forestry for the selection, management and protection of natural areas.

Leadership by foresters in setting aside natural areas is not surprising. In British Columbia, forestry is a leading industry. Pojar (1980) notes that some representative natural forest ecosystems are threatened with extinction in B.C., with the resulting loss of knowledge needed to prepare silvicultural interpretations and recommendations necessary to maintain a thriving forest industry.

The extinction of varieties and species of plants has

perhaps already occurred in B.C. (Myers 1979; Pojar 1980). The province's Ecological Reserves Program is intended to lessen future loss. While Provincial and Federal Parks may do the same thing, their priority is for recreation rather than native plant gene conservation.

The long term goal of the Ecological Reserves Program is to set aside an adequate sampling of the natural diversity of the province. Krajina (1976) estimates that this can be done in 0.5% of the land area of the province. Time will tell whether this is an accurate guess or not. It is impossible to predict the needs of mankind a century away. By then the options for setting aside additional natural areas will probably long since have passed.

The Ecological Reserves Act

The Act passed the Legislature unanimously in 1971. The major reasons for establishing Reserves are generally cited as follows:

1)   outdoor laboratories for research;
2)   "banks" of genetic material, nature museums containing rare species and genetically superior and marginal populations;
3)   benchmark areas, providing base-data of normality;
4)   outdoor classrooms.

The Ecological Reserves Act established the Ecological Reserves Program. At first, progress was made with the help of co-opted public servants and the public, particularly the staff of local universities. Then, in 1974, a Director (zoologist) was hired, followed by a plant ecologist, and later an assistant. The botanist is in charge of making new proposals for Reserves, while the assistant attempts to elminate conflicts in proposals as well as helping to manage Reserves. The Ecological Reserves Unit presently resides in the Ministry of Lands, Parks and Housing.

One hundred and three Ecological Reserves have been established on Crown land since the Act was passed, representing 113,905 hectares, or about 0.12% of the area of the Province. The staff of three had a total annual budget of about $120,000 in 1980-81. The Minister appoints an Advisory Board under Section 9 of the Act consisting of foresters, ecologists, lawyers, geologists, and naturalists, both inside and outside of government. Those appointed advise the Minister on matters relating to the establishment and administration of Ecological Reserves. The Act and

Regulations permit no mining, logging, hunting, fishing or
other extractive use of Reserves. Research is encouraged if
it does not significantly affect the possibility of future
researchers studying a natural area.

Establishing Ecological Reserves

British Columbia, with an area of 948,600 km^2, has been
divided into 12 biogeoclimatic zones by Krajina (1969).
These zones form a basis for selecting Ecological Reserve
proposals and are described by Krajina (1976) as "certain
ecosystems within a geographic region (in) which--similar
vegetation and soil are primarily products of similarities
in macroclimate and organismic phylogeny". The province's
flora comprises more than 50% of the vascular plant taxa in
Canada (Taylor and MacBryde, 1977) and therefore represents
the largest gene pool in the country.

Proposals for new Reserves must fit into a list of
needed representative plant community types, taking into
account what types have already been placed under Reserve
status. Triplicates or at least duplicates of types have
been deemed necessary from the beginning of the program to
mitigate against natural disasters which could destroy a
Reserve. Areas with unique plant or animal attributes are
also proposed. Representative Reserves will, of course,
tend to become unique with time as adjacent land uses alter
the natural environment.

While sometimes an informed member of the public makes
a proposal for an Ecological Reserve, generally the proposals are made by the three staff. With growing frequency,
members of the Research Division of the Ministry of Forests
make proposals.

Proposals generally are made on land owned by the
province (over 93% of the province is Crown land) since
there is no budget for acquiring private land. One parcel
of private land was donated and designated an Ecological
Reserve.

Once prepared, a proposal is referred to the provincial
government offices in the Regions to see whether there are
any conflicts with respect to potential dams, logging,
mining, hunting, fishing, etc. If there are no conflicts,
or if they can be resolved, a Reserve is created.

The most difficult Ecological Reserves to acquire - and
the most needed - are those with highly productive sites:

lowland forest, grasslands, and estuaries. Most are either degraded or committed to industry. Yet the need to preserve gene pools of "super" trees, intact grasslands and rich estuaries is obvious to many. Compensation to forest companies to acquire a forest committed to their use is very difficult; cattlemen are independent spirits who hotly defend every blade of grass for their cattle; and estuaries, even if they can be protected, are subject to the effects of any activity in the whole watershed and to adverse influences from marine traffic. Only occasionally can an entire small watershed be acquired, and the resulting estuary, if any, is small.

While Reserves are proposed usually for needed plant associations, sometimes the justification is related to specific genetic material. Thus the Chilliwack Reserve (86 ha) contains not only exceptional specimens of red cedar (Thuja plicata), grand fir (Abies grandis), silver fir (A. amabilis), sitka spruce (Picea sitchensis), and Engelmann spruce (P. engelmannii), but also hybrids between the two fir and between the two spruce species.

The 263 ha Reserve near Takla Lake contains the most northerly known occurrence of Douglas fir (Pseudotsuga menziesii). Genetically, this population is one of the most frost resistant; it could be used as a seed source for cold boreal regions.

The 188 ha Reserve near Clinton represents an Ecological Reserve of considerable economic importance to both forestry and agriculture. This Reserve contains a wide variety of herbaceous and woody plants belonging to the Interior Douglas-Fir biogeoclimatic zone. The Pinus ponderosa represents one of the northernmost populations of this tree species and thus may contain important hardiness genes of considerable value to tree-breeding programs. Of equal importance from an agronomic point of view are the several dryland forage grass species, e.g., Agropyron spicatum, Festuca idahoensis, Stipa comata and Calamagrostis rubescens. These populations of forage grasses could form an important breeding pool for selection and development of an indigenous grass-breeding program for revegetation of disturbed dry interior and prairie landscapes. Canada has not been overly active in the development of forage-breeding programs utilizing indigenous taxa and the preservation of significant gene pools of these grasses in Ecological Reserves provides a basis for long-term experimental programs in agronomy.

The potential of these gene pools cannot be immediately

known, but at least conserved genetic material is available for experimentation. Also of importance from an economic point of view are the reservoirs of potential commercial horticultural plant species and varieties as breeding resources. There are herbaceous plants and shrubs that can be used to develop hardy ornamental taxa for the nursery and landscape trade. Not only can these species be effective additions for ornamental purposes, but increasing attention is now being directed to the development of suitable indigenous plants for revegetation of large-scale disturbance sites, e.g., in dam construction, thermal projects, roads, strip mines and pipeline programs. An increasing concern by goverments and the public for re-establishing healthy, viable and appropriate vegetation on large-scale land disturbances highlights the significance of the Ecological Reserves Program in providing reservoirs of our native vegetation for research and experimental programs. The Reserves are true gene banks containing the diversity necessary for successful establishment and subsequent evaluation of plant breeding programs.

The Chilliwack, Takla Lake and Clinton Reserves represent examples of the economic potential of just three of the many Reserves that have been established. There is a need for both federal and provincial governments, as well as private research funding agencies, to establish specific funding policies for experimentation and evaluation of the potential gene pool resources in Reserves. These Reserves may well prove to be one of the most important conservation programs established, but there is an urgency to establish priorities and funding for long-term programs to achieve both scientific and economic benefits from the Ecological Reserves Program.

Management of Reserves

The goal for the management of the Reserves is the maintenance of genetic material and ecosystems by natural means. It is realized that most seral communities will eventually progress to a climax state, losing some species and gaining others in the process. Fire is the only management tool considered to be natural in some environments; eventually it may be used to attempt to maintain a Reserve in a seral stage.

Misuse of Ecological Reserves by the uninformed or unsympathetic public is commonplace. Fences are needed to keep out domestic stock, a public relations program to keep out all-terrain vehicles, and so on. A volunteer warden program is being established to help protect Reserves and to inform the public on the need for Reserves.

Research

There are two approaches to research in Ecological Reserves. One states that it is important to have baseline studies conducted in all Reserves as soon as possible. This would demonstrate to the public and politicians that Reserves are indeed needed. It will be impossible to return to the year 1981 once it is gone; perhaps in later years it will be very important to have baseline data on a given Reserve from the early 1980's, but such information cannot be gathered retrospectively.

The second approach states that the chief purpose of establishing Reserves is to put genetic material in a bank for future study and use to keep options open for future generations of mankind.

These two approaches are not contradictory and merely reflect different emphasis on the different purposes for Reserves.

In general, it is not possible to predict the sorts of questions to be answered by Reserves in later years, but without Reserves, the questions may not be answerable. The use of genetic conservation is often unpredictable; what will be needed—and when—cannot be itemized. The bottom line to Ecological Reserves is that extinction is forever; it behooves us to look after our genetic resources.

In British Columbia, while most Reserves were created for their plant associations, the bulk of the research has been on the wildlife (particularly seabirds) they contain. This will hopefully be remedied as the Research Division of the Ministry of Forests assumes a greater role.

Conclusions

The Ecological Reserves Program in British Columbia has made significant progress in establishing Ecological Reserves. However, the genetic material contained therein is often poorly known and resources for remedying this are minimal. In the meantime, misuse is degrading many Reserves.

Even the selection of proposed Reserves is not as scientific as one would like. The biotic diversity of such a huge area as the province overwhelms the few scientists available to quantify it. However, as options are running out daily as a result of irreversible land uses, action in genetic conservation cannot wait for the results of definitive studies.

The need for the preservation of genetic material is rising dramatically. Mankind is altering the face of the earth far faster than any other time in recorded history; a million species could go extinct between now and the end of the century (Myers 1979).

At the same time, conflict with existing Reserves is growing: more people, more leisure time, more all-terrain vehicles. Industry, once able to put a road anywhere in the hinterland, suddenly finds an Ecological Reserve in the middle of the cheapest proposed road location. The conflict continues.

Clearly, the most important job we have to do is to improve the political climate for the acceptance — and encouragement — of programs to preserve genetic material in natural reserves throughout the world.

Acknowledgements

The author extends his appreciation to Dr. Roy Taylor, Director, Botanical Gardens, University of British Columbia, Vancouver; Mr. Christopher Heamen and Dr. Jim Pojar, Research Division, Ministry of Forests; and to Dr. Hans Roemer, Ecological Reserves Unit, Ministry of Lands, Parks and Housing, Victoria, B.C., for helpful comments on the manuscript.

Literature Cited

Fosberg, R.F. 1981. An overview of natural area preservation in the world. In: Ecological Reserves, a symposium of the 13th Pacific Science Congress. B.C. Prov. Museum Heritage Record 12. Victoria, B.C. pp. 1-6.

Krajina, V.J., 1969. Ecology of forest trees in British Columbia. Dept. Bot., U.B.C., Vancouver, B.C., Canada. Ecol. Western N.A. 2: 1-146.

Krajina, V.J., 1976. Progress of Ecological Reserves in British Columbia. Proceedings Symp. Can. Bot. Assn. 13th Ann. Meet. pp. 15-21.

McLaren, I.A., and E.B. Peterson, 1975. Ecological Reserves in Canada: The Work of IBP-CT. Nature Canada 4: 22-32.

Myers, N.   1979.   The sinking ark.   Pergamon Press. 307 pp.

Pojar, J. 1980. Threatened forest ecosystems of British Columbia.   In: Threatened and Endangered Species and Habitats in British Columbia and the Yukon.   Fish and Wildlife   Branch,   B.C.   Ministry   of   Environment. pp. 28-39.

Romancier, R.M., 1974. Natural area programs. Jour. For. 72: 37-42.

Taylor, R.L., and Bruce MacBryde, 1977. Vascular plants of British Columbia: a descriptive resource inventory. Tech. Bull. No. 4, the Botanical Garden of U.B.C., Vancouver. The University of British Columbia Press.

Weetman, G.F., 1972. Canadian Institute of Forestry policy for selection, protection and management of natural areas. For. Chron. 48: 41-43.

7. Policies, Strategies, and Means for Genetic Conservation in Forestry

The maintenance of genetic diversity is fully as important for forestry as it is in general agriculture (FAO/UNEP 1975). It is an accepted concept that there must be an active and vigorous program for the protection and conservation of the basic agricultural crops and their progenitors if modern agriculture is to meet world food needs. Such efforts are constantly receiving serious attention by the agricultural community and have a general acceptance by the public (National Academy of Sciences 1972). Similar efforts to conserve the forest genetic heritage are less well understood by both the public and the scientific community. Yet, appropriate management of the genetic resource is just as essential if forestry is to be responsive to changing social needs and public aspirations (National Academy of Sciences 1972).

It remains the goal of forest management to produce a broad array of forest products and services on a sustained basis. Furthermore, the types of forest products needed will vary both in time and place. The modern forester must employ management strategies that maintain a reliable and highly varied genetic reservoir for future use and possible genetic improvement. In addition, means must also be provided for insuring and perpetuating selected large and small populations for future mass seed production to meet unforseen contingencies (Maini, Yeatman and Teich 1975; Yeatman 1972). In modern forestry we cannot readily control the environmental events that shape our long-lived forest stands. However, unlike agriculture, forestry still has the natural resources to achieve these goals if we act promptly (Barber and Krugman 1974; Maini 1973).

There is an urgent need to have a vigorous program now for maintaining ancestral forest tree lines as well as a

71

broad genetic base both for current as well as future genetic selection and forest tree improvement programs. Maintaining an adequate diversity of the forest genetic resource provides an opportunity to respond to natural catastrophies by restoring forest stands. This same genetic diversity is also needed for developing new combinations to produce individuals that are better adapted to specific environmental situations and thus make it possible for a reduced land base to support a more productive forest under intensive forest management (Franklin 1979; Yeatman 1972).

Forest History and Practice

To understand the opportunities in the United States for the management of the genetic resource for forest lands, especially those administered by the USDA Forest Service, it is first necessary to appreciate the history of these lands and how forestry differs from general agriculture.

Historically, there was some loss of genetic material as the United States was settled but the degree of this loss and genetic disturbance varied in their intensity in different parts of the country. In the eastern portions of the United States there was extensive land clearing and considerable disturbance to portions of the native forests. Highgrading, the removal of only the best trees or selected species, was a common practice. In the southern pine belt, land clearing for agriculture was followed by land abandonment which led to stands established from parental stands of often narrow genetic origin (Franklin 1979). In some cases, we suspect that natural regeneration was followed by a high degree of inbreeding, since relatively few seed parents remained. This was later followed in some southern areas by a high degree of offsite plantings (McConnell 1980). In the western United States, forest use has had a much smaller impact except in certain local areas of high utilization or disturbance. However, the situation in the West is rapidly changing with the removal of the last old growth natural stands. Although such stands are commonly replaced by natural seedlings of local seed origin, there is often some genetic selection in the regeneration material and a narrowing of the original genetic base. Even now, most forest stands in the United States are still reestablished by local natural regeneration.

With a few exceptions, current forest plantings are not derived from exotic germ plasm or from crops derived from material that has been selected over many generations (Barber and Krugman 1974). Only a limited amount of genetically-improved material is available and none of this is far removed from the wild type. Only a relatively small portion of federal lands are involved in intensive forest management with large planting programs. Even the current pine and Douglas-fir plantations are produced from cross-pollinated seeds from a number of parents and are, in fact, diverse in their genetic make-up. Currently it is still possible, if needed, to return to the original gene pool to pick up added genetic diversity (Silen and Doig 1976).

Management Issues

Even though current management practices have had only a limited impact on the genetic resource, serious attention must still be directed toward preventing possible future problems. As forest management becomes more intensive in those areas designated to produce wood products, a program of conservation spruce must be available and in place to prevent losses in the genetic resource. Furthermore, forestry must be sensitive to changing needs and to changes in the land resource available to it. At least in parts of the United States, especially in the southern portions of the country, some of the current forested area will once again be converted to traditional agriculture and forest management will be restricted to the more marginal lands.

If forest uses are uncontrolled or if ill-managed and natural forest gene pools mixed indiscriminately, selected natural gene pools will soon become impoverished or even eliminated. There are still problems associated with some offsite plantings, but this issue can best be addressed by implementing existing guidelines on the proper choice of seed source for a given area. A more immediate concern is the destruction of a valuable genetic source during the normal harvesting operation. This can only be addressed by a genetic resource management program which is an integral part of the forest management program.

What then are the current programs now underway to protect the forest genetic resource and are these programs adequate? The bases of the current Forest Service effort rest on a knowledge and appreciation for the (1) nature of past, current, and expected land use and pressure on the genetic resource, i.e., degree of past genetic disturbance; (2) current level of understanding of the genetic resource, i.e., degree of genetic variation and differentiation; and (3) extent and scope of the natural range of the species or species complex.

Management Strategies

The Forest Service has, as needed, a rapid response system for clearly identifiable conservation or protection needs. Unique populations and threatened or endangered species or populations can quickly be placed under genetic resource management by establishing such a population as a Research Natural Area, Botanical Area, or special use area. Use and activities in such areas are carefully regulated and controlled. Although these units are most commonly employed to protect ecosystems, they can be used to protect small or large populations as well. Over 400 such areas have now been established. Large populations have also been placed under essentially genetic resource management by virtue of their special use or function. Wilderness areas, recreation areas, roadside strips and scenic areas can all be managed to protect and maintain a given genetic resource (Theisen 1980). More recently, the Forest Service has added the Biosphere Reserve designation to selected areas. These forest reserves represent special areas of natural forest ecosystems in which both static and dynamic management can be applied. To be effective as a genetic management unit, a Biosphere Reserve must include forest ecosystems which are representative of the forest gene resource commonly found in areas where forest management is practiced or other pressures may seriously modify the genetic composition (Krugman 1979; Krugman and Phares 1978).

The most serious concern to the long-term management of the forest genetic resource is how to maintain the genetic resource subject to intensive or even extensive forest management. It is in these areas that the genetic resources are under the most serious pressure. It is here that type conversions are most likely to occur with a rapid change in species and genetic composition. It is in these areas of intensive forest management that there is the greatest reluctance to set aside additional areas for nontimber production purposes.

Most set-aside areas, i.e., Research Natural Areas and Wilderness Areas represent the unique or unusual. The extremes of the species range are most commonly protected by the establishment of special use areas. A new system of specially identified areas, Genetic Resource Management Units, is being considered to conserve the gene resource in stands under active forest management and still permit the stand to meet management production goals. Fortunately, there are available several silvicultural strategies which permit normal use of the forest and, with certain management modifications, continuation of the greatest genetic diversity.

Natural Regeneration Systems. In those forest stands where the natural regeneration systems are adequately known (and such is the case for most United States species), it is possible by modifying current harvesting systems to provide a sufficient number, distribution and type of parent or seed trees to insure an adequate and broad genetic base in selected representative areas. In those forest types in which the next generation is best provided by advanced natural regeneration already present in the understory, by modifying the current placement and size of the logging and road systems an adequate understory of the appropriate species mix can be maintained which will represent the basic genetic structure of the original stand. However, it is still necessary to have a backup system. This can be accomplished by the establishment of representative stands that are maintained for seed production and thus can provide seeds of locally adapted populations. When needed, and if necessary, ex situ areas can be established with representative samples of the natural populations if such stands cannot now be maintained under the natural regeneration system. Other ex situ methods such as seed collection and storage to protect a genetic resource in the short term can also be employed if there is a doubt that the population can be maintained under essentially natural conditions.

Artificial Regeneration Systems. In those management areas in which artificial regeneration systems are the most appropriate, and where genetically-improved material is not planted, then local seed sources should be used. Such local seed sources should be representative of the forest conditions and reflect the normal as well as the possible unique conditions or niches commonly found in the forest situation. Source of this seed can come from the stands prior to their harvesting, or from representative seed production stands in the harvesting area.

Genetic Resource Management Unit. Where intensive management is being or will be practiced using genetically-improved material, then Genetic Resource Management Units should be identified and established in the area under management. A Genetic Resource Management Unit is a representative area maintained in which only local seed sources are used and disgenic selection practices are avoided, i.e., the removal of the best trees or the removal of certain species or size classes is avoided. Thus essentially normal forest uses and management practices can be conducted. It is only essential to maintain a high degree of natural genetic diversity.

Not all forest management areas need to have Genetic Resources Management Units; but, sufficient areas should be so identified as to fully represent the forest genetic complex.

Under these management practices, species currently not being utilized in forest production would still be protected and maintained. However, it is recognized that some of these species complexes must be maintained in special use areas, i.e., Research Natural Areas, Parks and Botanical Areas. As noted before, stress populations would be included under this heading.

Other Genetic Resource Needs. In addition, there are some species or seed sources that are currently of limited importance to the United States but are of interest to forestry programs in other countries. Such is the case with Monterey pine (Pinus radiata D. Don) and numerous seed sources of a number of our commercial and noncommercial tree species. It is our responsibility, within the limits of our resources, to protect and maintain these species or seed sources. This material could be best maintained in Genetic Resource Management Units. Such genetic material could be also protected in special areas where use is under strict management control and conservation of the genetic component of the resource has a high priority. To ensure the continuation of certain populations, it is still necessary also to include ex situ methods including special stand establishment, clonal archives, collection and storage of seeds, and perhaps, in time, tree tissues. These latter practices currently are not as widely employed in forestry as is common in agriculture but the necessary methodology is being developed.

We are in the process of developing appropriate guidelines for the identification and establishment of Genetic Resource Management Units. Such units should be established in all National Forests in order to encompass as much of the biological and environmental variation as feasible. Such areas are to be of sufficient size to minimize the hazard of foreign pollen contamination.

Such reserves should include typical representative stands of a local area as well as those highly unique and exceptional in growth and form. The management strategies employed in the individual Genetic Resource Management Units will tend to be conservative but will reflect the current state of knowledge. In some cases there will be an attempt to manage shade intolerant species by interventions, i.e., fire, logging, and planting. The Genetic Resource Management Units will provide a reliable and varied genetic reservoir for conserving and perpetuating selected populations for forestry and related uses and still permit other appropriate uses of these same areas. In those areas in which the genetic resource has been already seriously depleted then a directed selection, breeding and planting program should be initiated in an attempt to restore adapted species mixtures.

The Forest Service administers only a portion of the forest lands of the United States. In eastern United States, where very little of the forest resource will be covered by the proposed program, the conservation needs are the greatest. It is hoped that other federal and state forest resource agencies, as well as private forestry companies, will join in a cooperative effort of forest genetic resource conservation and the program will become national in scope.

Literature Cited

Barber, J.C., and S.L. Krugman. 1974. Preserving forest tree germ plasm. Am. For. 80(1): 8-11.

FAO/UNEP. 1975. Report on a pilot study on the methodology of conservation of forest genetic resources. FO Misc. 75-8. 117 pp.

Franklin, E.C. 1979. High hopes for native pines. Am. Forests 85(10): 24-27.

Krugman, S.L. 1979. Biosphere Reserves - Strategies for the Conservation and Management of Forest Gene Pool Resources. In: Selection, Management and Utilization of Biosphere Reserves, J.F. Franklin and S.L. Krugman, Eds. U.S. Department of Agriculture Forest Service General Technical Report PNW-82. pp. 123-127.

Krugman, S.L. and R.E. Phares. 1978. Use and management of Biosphere Reserves of the Man and Biosphere program for environmental monitoring and conservation. FQL-26-4 Eighth World Forestry Congress, Jakata. 16 pp.

McConnell, J.L. 1980. The southern forest - past, present and future. In: Proceedings Servicewide Workshop on Gene Resource Management, U.S. Department of Agriculture, Forest Service, Timber Management. pp. 17-26.

Maini, J.S.   1973.   Conservation of forest tree gene resources in Canada: An ecological perspective.   In: Proceedings of the Thirteenth Meeting of the Committee on Forest Tree Breeding in Canada, Part 2, D.P. Fowler and C.W. Yeatman, eds.   Can. For. Serv., Ottawa, Canada. pp. 43-50.

Maini, J.S., C.W. Yeatman, and A.H. Teich.   1975.   In situ and Ex situ Conservation of gene resources of Pinus banksiana and Picea glauca.   FAO Report on Pilot Study on Methodology of Conservation of Forest Genetic Resources FO MISC 75-8.   pp. 27-40.

National Academy of Sciences. 1972.   Genetic vulnerability of major crops.   Report of National Academy of Sciences, Washington, D.C.   307 pp.

Silen, R.R. and I. Doig.   1976.   The care and handling of the forest gene pool.   Pacific Search 10(8): 7-9.

Theisen, P.A.   1980.   Maintenance of genetic diversity and gene pool conservation of commercial or potentially commercial tree species in the Pacific Northwest Region United States Forest Service.   In. Proc. Servicewide Workshop on Gene Resource Management, U.S. Department of Agriculture, Forest Service, Timber Management. pp. 61-186.

Yeatman, C.W.   1972.   Gene pool conservation for applied breeding and seed production.   Proceedings IUFRO Genetics- SABRAO Joint Symposia, Tokyo, pp. B-8(V), I-B-8(V),6.

8. Strategies for Gene Conservation in Forest Tree Breeding

When applied to forest trees, the concept of conservation is commonly confounded with that of preservation. In this paper, the objective of gene conservation is restricted to improving the usefulness of trees for various forms of human consumption. While achieving improving usefulness may require preservation of sets of genotypes, maintenance of genotypes, populations, or species for their own sake is more properly considered elsewhere (Frankel 1974). Gene conservation can contribute to breeding by providing allelic variations for advanced generation development but these benefits are not realized for a long time and private or public investors in breeding programs require reasonable rates of return. Thus, even if genes are readily available in some resource population, there are economic problems in conserving them for long-term breeding. These problems are compounded when the genes exist in relatively poorly adapted varieties and must be introduced into commercially competitive varieties (Stuber 1978). For many crop species, the economic and biological problems are not insurmountable but for forest tree species the problems are different and their solution requires multiple breeding stategies.

Some Salient Features of Forest Trees

Per unit of area occupied, the aggregate value of forests and the products they yield is normally lower than that of agronomic species. As a result, forests generally occupy areas that are unsuitable for other economic crop production under the local conditions. Since forest sites tend to be infertile, remote, or physically difficult to manage, both economic and biological constraints on forestry and forest tree breeding are considerable.

Forest conditions are extremely variable in almost all respects, and the tree breeder must take these variations into account. Pine breeding for tropical forest plantations is far different from poplar breeding for the Mississippi Valley, and both differ from spruce breeding for boreal forests. Some species have relatively short breeding cycles and short harvest rotations, while others may require two decades for a breeding cycle and a century for a timber rotation. It makes as much sense to lump all forest trees into a single class of organisms as to lump all agronomic crops. While variations cannot be ignored, it is my purpose here to look at some common features of forest trees and to make some conclusions about active tree breeding programs. My conclusions are most applicable to tree breeding in temperate North America.

The accumulating evidence, largely with temperate zone conifer species, indicates that genetic variation in tree species is relatively high among plant species (Yeh 1979). Tree populations have not been as genetically decimated as some agronomic species, and the high level of allelic variations indicates the presence of a substantial reservoir of usable genotypic variation. In North America, indigenous populations are available for initiating breeding programs. Hence, we can often start with biologically well adapted populations which contain substantial variability. Also, existing technology for genotype storage makes preservation relatively easy. Not only can seeds be stored for long periods, but individual trees can grow well for many decades, and cloning can often be used to store genotypes in multiple propagules.

For all of these advantages, however, gene conservation is a substantial problem in forestry. The above advantages are not universally available and the time scale of operations mitigates against long-term gene management. Economic pressures for early returns inhibit investments in long-term forest gene conservation. The rate of loss of natural forests throughout the world is rapid in critical areas (Spears 1979), and there is an attendant loss of populations and alleles and little conservation activity. In situ forest reserves for ecosystem conservation have been recommended (UNESCO 1973), but they are difficult to initiate and maintain (FAO 1975). To some extent, ex situ conservation stands supplement these efforts for species of proven industrial commercial value. In these commercially important species, either small selected samples are used in breeding, or large gene pool conservation stands are established (Burley and Namkoong 1980). To provide for long-term needs, forestry breeding programs have emphasized two contrasting operational modes. In a few programs, the emphasis is on intensive breeding in closed populations which may be supplemented in future generations by genotypes from previously unselected populations (Zobel 1977). In some others, especially where the natural populations are insecure, the emphasis is on establishing a large gene pool of about 10,000 trees which is preserved with little selection to serve as a permanent source of genetic heterogeneity for any future breeding (Marshall and Brown 1975; Whitmore 1977). While the relative efficiences of these alternates are debatable (Zobel 1978), both rely on undomesticated, base populations as sources of new genotypes for future breeding. Since these populations contain enough genetic variation to provide immediate genetic improvements, there is a sense of security that as long as undomesticated populations exist or genotypes are stored as seeds or clones, we can always return to wild, base populations for future genetic improvements. A closer examination of the premise of security, however, reveals that such unimproved base populations are an illusory refuge and that preserved genotypes will be relatively useless in advanced tree breeding programs.

Substantial gains from simple breeding programs have been demonstrated for most forest tree species (Zobel 1978), and there can be little reasonable doubt that land productivity can be substantially advanced by the direct effects of breeding for wood yield. In addition, there are indirect effects of breeding which increase the land base on which commercial forestry may be practiced, such as breeding for juvenile survival and growth on otherwise submarginal lands. Over large areas, such breeding can have substantial economic impact. Of equal importance is the reduction of time from planting to harvest.

All these gains, however, are achieved over relatively long periods from breeding to commercial payoff. The pressures for immediate and rapid progress virtually prohibit investing in programs with poorly defined advanced generation benefits. If it is difficult for breeders of annual crops to justify breeding programs with long-term payoffs, then the difficulties of tree breeders are another order of magnitude greater. At least 5 years, and more commonly 10 to 20 years, are required to complete a generational cycle from seed to seed, and 20 to 80 years from planting to harvest. Hence, tree breeders must direct their efforts to environments and markets of a distant and uncertain future, and carry investment costs for very long periods.

In most first generation efforts, a base breeding

population is developed by recurrent selection with 10 to 50 parents (Pederick and Griffin 1977). A subset of these is used in seed production orchards for current planting needs. In the recurrent selection program, up to 50 selected parents may be partially intercrossed and the progeny generation selected on the basis of family performances for general combining ability (Kellison and Dinus 1977). This type of family selection rapidly reduces the effective population size but expected gain is high since the family heritability is high and the selection differential in these first generations is high. Increasing the population size in the breeding populations inevitably reduces not only the selection differential but also the heritability, since the estimation error is hard to control in large experiments. The temptation to use the few best genotypes to advance the breeding population is enormous, even with full recognition that by so doing, gains in subsequent generations may be forfeited. Forest tree breeders are thus forced to adopt a breeding strategy that involves little cumulative population development. They will have to return to unimproved genotypes at frequent generational intervals and at considerable cost in long-term gain. Consider that at current rates of improvement of 15-20% per generation (or 1-2% per year), the improved populations can yield about half again as much in three generations as now.

By that time, any unimproved genotypes which we may wish to introduce into the breeding populations will require special and rapid breeding efforts to be of any economic benefit. While the generation lag may be small, the time lag is large and the economic benefit of using unimproved, preserved genotypes is low. Hence, the use of unimproved genotypes will be limited to the first few generations of breeding because the cost of using them will be high and the time required to develop new varieties will be too long to justify investment. Clearly, conservation cannot remain separate from breeding, and it cannot be judged solely on the basis of current economic utility.

Conservation and Breeding Programs

Initially, tree breeding programs were developed with highly selected, small populations. Especially with introduced species, early efforts were concentrated on finding the single best source populations and selecting a few best of the parents for seed production orchards (Langlet 1963). For native species, the diversity of populations was more often maintained in separate breeding programs in which a local source population was used in

each.   With an increased awareness that selection would
rapidly reduce the effective population size, several
programs initiated breeding with a few hundred trees (Burdon
et al. 1977), while others reselected in natural or planted
stands to increase the base populations to several hundred
for each regionally adapted breeding population.

While these population sizes should be sufficient for
long-term breeding, the pressures for rapid gain and
restricted population sizes previously cited are being felt.
Most programs develop one population per physiographic zone
while some cooperative programs maintain separate breeding
populations but exchange parental genotypes among those
populations (Nikles and Burley 1977).   Furthermore, most of
these programs with substantial initial population sizes
include progeny test selection plans for culling the next
generation to well less than 50 of the original selected
trees.   Further reductions by family and pedigree selection
are usually mentioned in breeding plans for the next few
generations (Kellison and Dinus 1977), and selection and
mating designs that maintain effective population sizes
greater than 50 are rare (Van Bujtenen and Lowe 1979;
Namkoong et al. 1980).

Since breeding agencies must justify program costs with
near-term genetic gains, dilution of a generation's gain by
including less immediately valuable genotypes in the
breeding population is extremely difficult.   Even for those
programs which split their populations into a smaller, more
highly selected set for current reforestation seed production and a larger set for generating the next breeding
population, pressures will persist to reduce the breeding
population in order to increase the rate of gain in both the
breeding and its derived seed production populations.
Therefore, unless deliberately planned and independently
supported, gene conservation will not be effective in aiding
breeding programs.

Population Structures

One possible solution exists in separating populations
more completely by carrying hierarchies of populations with
long- and short-term objectives (Kannenberg, 1984).   These
hierarchies can be compared with more traditional agricultural breeding organizations which develop commercial
varieties from breeders' populations.   The base of these
hierarchies usually originates in State or Federal
Experiment Stations or private organizations which carry
collections of lines, or varieties, which can be intermated
to form new recombinants or breeding populations.   Since

exotic germplasms can be added to these populations, gene conservation programs have direct means for affecting established varieties as described elsewhere in this volume. As promising new varieties are developed, standard testing procedures provide certifiable results and the seed stock can be expanded for producing the successful entries. International organizations like CIMMYT, have similar hierarhcies of breeding populations with a large base of genotypes feeding into selected breeding populations which may be more specifically adapted for use.

For forest tree species, hierarchies have been proposed (Namkoong et al. 1971) with large base breeding populations being either unimproved collections of diverse source, or mildly selected for survival and growth on some sites. This approach may not be feasible for forest tree breeding. The problem is that if these populations do not improve at nearly the same rate as the more highly selected commercial varieties, use of these populations will cause substantial declines in yield. If these base populations are preserved rather than improved, they will remain relatively useless in advanced breeding programs and will be useful only in the event of disasters which they may be fortunate enough to escape and if they possess otherwise lost alleles. To ensure their use in such circumstances, populations must be very large and management for diversity must be almost as intensive as that for immediate gain in advanced breeding populations. Low-intensity selection in base populations with the same general objectives as the high-intensity selection for commercial varieties only partially assuages the problem. Since the degree of amelioration depends on the level of advance in base populations, the same pressures for rapid advance apply to the base population as well as the commercial varieties. It may be argued that base populations can be selected for a basic set of adaptabilities, leaving sufficient allelic variability for future breeding of special adaptabilities. It is more likely, however, that specialized adaptabilities would be foregone in favor of more rapid advance in basic adaptabilities. Therefore, there is little cost advantage to maintaining a hierarchial structure with unimproved or moderately improved base breeding populations as contrasted with active breeding programs. Hence, gene conservation by means of hierarchies of breeding populations is not likely to be viable for active forest tree breeding.

However, if active breeding programs are affordable and the pressures for immediate gains are substantial, gene conservation can be incorporated into forest tree breeding programs by constructing multiple sets of breeding populations. Instead of constructing hierarchies of breeding populations or hierarchies of traits and environmental objectives, the objectives for breeding populations can be factored into components of site adaptabilities and trait variables. Within the space defined by the factored variables, different sets of optimum selection coefficients can be defined for expected future needs or, more conservatively, for minimax gain under conditions of environmental or economic uncertainty. Multiple index selection sets (MISS) may be defined and multiple subpopulations can be separately bred for diverse objectives (Namkoong 1976). The more uniformly and narrowly defined the set of objective functions, the less the need is for diversity among sets and this strategy degenerates to the replicate population concept of Baker and Curnow (1969). However, the greater the diversity of objective functions, or the greater the uncertainty of future needs, the greater is the benefit of diverse subpopulations since some few of them would have a greater probability of being close to the optimum than a single population would. In addition, if disease or insect resistance programs require genetic diversity of forest stands, diversity can more easily be designed by mixing divergent populations in plantations than by homogenizing resistance mechanisms in single varieties.

For any given species and for any given total population size, the choice of number of subpopulations and effective number per subpopulation is affected by the costs of maintaining separate breeding groups and the loss rate of useful alleles in small population breeding. For forest trees, I estimate that a maximum population size of 10 to 20 should be maintained in each of 20 to 50 or more subpopulations, for diverse species. Within each subpopulation, simple recurrent selection is the expected norm. Hybridization among subpopulations may involve some forms of modified reciprocal recurrent selection, or the hybrids may simply generate new subpopulations for advanced generation simple recurrent selection. Programs of this size are not much larger than current breeding programs and require about the same effort as hierarchically organized programs.

Gene conservation is quite different in a multiple population breeding structure than in a hierarchical breeding structure; in the former case, it is an integral part of breeding population management. The emphasis on maintaining diversity is placed on interpopulational structures instead of merely assuring the presence of alleles within a hierarchy of base populations with its attendant problems of

effectively using such alleles in breeding. <u>As a part of</u>
<u>breeding population management, gene conservation implies</u>
<u>much more than preserving one generation's allelic array.</u>
<u>In this context, gene conservation is identical to long-term</u>
<u>breeding or populational gene management and implies wide</u>
<u>population sampling as a start for designed multiplicity,</u>
<u>and continued development of population diversity as</u> envi-
ronmental and economic demands change.

Program Structures

Since most forestry agencies deal with several species,
their gene management programs can vary in form and
intensity. For species and populations with high present
value, there is little problem in developing programs which
satisfy immediate commercial breeding objectives and
long-term gene conservation objectives. In the next one or
two generations, either hierarchical or multiple factor
populations can satisfy short- and long-term objectives as
long as population sizes are kept large. The divergence in
utility of the programs will occur soon after that.   Of
greater concern for long-term gene management are those
species or populations with low apparent present value, with
which breeding will be done on a small scale. The concern
with such low priority species is that they may fill some
future needs but that we will have lost useful alleles and
populations due to poor genetic husbandry.   For such
species, it may be impractical and, by present best
estimates, a waste of resources to breed many subpopulations. The maximum affordable program may well be to test
and develop one small breeding population intensively while
preserving or minimally selecting the other populations.
Multiple source populations are preferable, but if only one
such minimally selected base population can be afforded, it
should be kept large and the program degenerates to a
two-stage hierarchy with one or a very few commercially
developed populations.

At present budgeting levels, most breeding agencies
must limit intensive efforts to a few species. Thus, most
tree species are treated in low priority programs with
single small populations used for commercial variety
development. These are not usually budgeted at a level to
ensure the storage or conservation of multiple source
populations, and only if several agencies maintain independent breeding populations will any useful diversity be
maintained. Even for such species as may deserve high
intensity effort, current breeding programs tend to reduce
effective population sizes.

If, as in agronomic breeding, single agencies are not likely to fund long-term gene management, the development of future tree breeding populations must rely on interagency organizations. Unfortunately, there are no national or international programs to direct or coordinate gene resource development for breeding populations among agencies. There are some federal programs to preserve genetic diversity (Theisen 1980) by setting aside designated areas, mostly in preserves. There are also state heritage programs for preservation, and a few notable exceptions in breeding programs which clearly plan for interpopulational diversity as a breeding plan. But by and large, however, gene conservation is not an effective part of breeding programs. Private industries cannot reasonably be expected to afford programs for other than immediate gain, state governments have not budgeted such programs, and the federal forest management agencies have not been charged with responsibility for overall gene mangement of any forest tree species. Internationally, the FAO concentrates its efforts on influencing national forestry programs to include conservation activities, and the Commonwealth Forestry Institute provides program guidance for some tropical pine species. However, the international agencies do not have enough funds to invest heavily in breeding programs. Without national directives for gene management, any useful gene conservation programs for tree breeding are individual efforts. Thus, while the marginal costs of good gene conservation programs are minimal, foresters lack the organizational structures which are available for other crops to ensure gene conservation in breeding programs. Such organizations should not be difficult to generate since forest conservation organizations already exist. What is required is a deepening of the concepts of conservation to the genetic level. If gene conservaton means the wise use of genetic resources, and forest conservation means the wise use of forest resources, gene conservation is requisite for forest conservation and forest tree breeding.

Literature Cited

Baker, L.H., and R.N. Curnow. 1969. Choice of population size and use of variation between replicate populations in plant breeding selection programs. Crop Sci. 9: 555-560.

Burdon, R., C. Shelbourne, and M. Wilcox. 1977. Advanced selection strategies. Proceedings Third World Consultation on Forest Tree Breeding, 2. pp. 1133-1147.

Burley, J. and G. Namkoong. 1980. Conservation of forest

genetic resources. Proceedings of the 11th Commonwealth Forestry Conference. 25 pp. (Mimeo)

F.A.O. 1975. Methodology of Conservation of Forest Genetic Resources. FAO/UNEP. Rome. 127 pp.

Frankel, O.H. 1974. Genetic conservation our evolutionary responsibility. Genetics 78: 53-65.

Frankel, O.H. 1977. Philosophy and strategy of genetic conservation in plants. Proceedings Third World Consultation on Forest Tree Breeding, 1. pp. 6-11.

Kannenberg, L.W. 1984. Utilization of genetic diversity in crop breeding. (This volume).

Kellison, R.C. and R.J. Dinus. 1977. Recent advances in genetic improvement of Pinus taeda and Pinus elliotii in the northern United States. Proceedings Third World Consultation on Forest Tree Breeding, 2. pp. 475-488.

Langlet, O. 1963. Practical results and current problems in provenance research in Sweden. Proceedings World Consultation on Forest Genetics and Tree Improvement, 1, Sect. 3: 1-10.

Marshall, D.R. and A.H.D. Brown. 1975. Optimum sampling strategies in genetic conservation. In Crop genetic resources for today and tomorrow (O.H. Frankel and I.G. Hawkes, eds.) IBP2, Cambridge University Press, Cambridge. pp. 53-80.

Namkoong, G. 1976. A multiple-index selection strategy. Silvae Genet. 25: 199-201.

Namkoong, G., R.D. Barnes, and J. Burley. 1980. A Philosophy of Breeding Strategies for Tropical Forest Trees. Tropical Forestry Papers, Univ. of Oxford. 67 pp.

Namkoong, G., R.C. Biesterfeldt, and J.C. Barber. 1971. Tree breeding and management decisions. J. For. 69: 138-142.

Nikles, D.G. and J. Burley. 1977. International cooperation in breeding tropical pines. Proceedings Third World Consultation on Forest Tree Breeding, 2. pp. 1157-1186.

Pederick, L.A. and A.R. Griffin. 1977. The genetic improvement of radiata pine in Australisia. Proceedings

Third World Consultation on Forest Tree Breeding, 2. pp. 561-572.

Silen, R. 1966. A simple progressive tree improvement program for Douglas-fir. Pacific Northwest Forest Exp. Sta. Res. Note 45. 13 pp.

Spears, J.S. 1979. Can the wet tropical forest survive? Commonw. For. Rev. 58(3): 165-180.

Stuber, C.W. 1978. Exotic sources for broadening genetic diversity in corn breeding programs. In Thirty-Third Annual Corn and Sorghum Research Conf. pp. 34-467.

Theisen, P.A. 1980. Maintenance of genetic diversity and gene pool conservation of commercial or potentially commercial tree species in the Pacific Northwest Region United States Forest Service. In Proceedings Service-wide Workshop on Gene Resource Management. USDA Forest Service, Timber Management. pp. 61-186.

UNESCO. 1973. Conservation of natural areas and the genetic material they contain. Rept. Expert Panel MAB Proj. 8, UNESCO, Paris. 64 pp.

Van Bujtenen, J.P. and W.J. Lowe. 1979. The use of breeding groups in advanced generation breeding. In Proceedings 15th Southern Forest Tree Improvement Conf. pp. 59-65.

Whitmore, T.C. 1977. A first look at Agathis. Trop. For. Pap. No. 11, CFI, Oxford. 54 pp.

Yeh, F.C. 1979. The role of isozyme research in tree improvement. Proceedings 17th Meeting Canadian Tree Improvement Ass. pp. 101-108.

Zobel, B. 1977. Gene conservation - as viewed by a forest tree breeder. For. Ecol. Management 1: 339-344.

Zobel, B. 1978. The good life or subsistence: some benefits of tree breeding. Unasylva 30: 5-9.

Part 3

Genetic Conservation in Breeding Crop-Plants

9. Utilization of Genetic Diversity in Crop Breeding

Crop Diversity

Duvick (1977) has summarized the extent of cultivar diversity in the major crops of the United States. The U.S. situation would be typical of most agriculturally advanced countries. Some U.S. crops are represented for the most part by only a few cultivars. For example, Upland cotton is predominated by 6 varietal types, the various types of wheat by 2-4 cultivars each, and peanuts by 4 cultivars with one cultivar accounting for 60% of total production. Some of the apomictic or vegetatively reproduced forage grasses also are represented by a few widely grown homogeneous cultivars. There are about 10 cultivars of red clover, 5 or 6 of white clover, and only one of crimson clover (Taylor et al. 1977). Other crops may be represented by a relatively large number of cultivars but their genetic base is in fact restricted. For example, literally hundreds of corn hybrids are grown in the United States and Canada, but these are based overwhelmingly on about a dozen inbred lines (Goodman and McK.Bird 1977).

Most of the cultivars grown today in developed countries are the products of continual recycling of materials originating from a few germplasm sources. Essentially, breeders use the current best cultivars or lines as parent stocks for the next generation of cultivars and then repeat the process. The net effect is a continuing constriction of the genetic base, a base which was none too broad to begin with. For example, the major cultivars of hard red winter wheat trace back to just two cultivars, Turkey and Marquis (Duvick 1977). The predominant North American cultivars of malting barley include, at the most, 11 outside sources of germplasm (Eslick and Hockett 1974). Soybean cultivars are derived from 12 strains from a small

area in northeastern China (Duvick 1977) and the most widely
used U.S. and Canadian cultivars involve at least one of the
old cultivars Richland and Mandarin in their parentage
(Hartwig 1973). Most hybrid sorghum cultivars involve just
two original cultivars and only one cytoplasm (Webster
1976). All present U.S. alfalfa varieties originate from 9,
albeit diverse, sources of germplasm and most new varieties
have been developed by recombining selections from previous
varieties (Barnes 1980). The American hybrid corn industry
is based on inbred lines from a few open-pollinated
varieties of a single race out of the 170 to 200 races
(extrapolated from Goodman and McK.Bird 1977) known in
maize.

Genetic Erosion

Risks. The hazards of such genetic uniformity have
been emphasized repeatedly (e.g., Marshall 1977, Committee
on Genetic Vulnerability of Major Crops 1972, Harlan
1972). The immediate hazard, and the one which has received
by far the most attention, is the increased vulnerability of
genetically uniform crops to insect or disease epidemics.
There is the potential for the disease or insect to rage out
of control on thousands of acres of a uniformly susceptible
host. The hazard is real, as evidenced by such modern
epidemics as Victoria blight on oats, the recurrent attacks
of leaf and stem rust on wheat and oats, Southern corn leaf
blight,[1] bacterial speck in tomatoes, alfalfa weevil, and
greenbug on sorghum. A major part of many breeding programs
involves searching for genes conferring resistance to new
disease races and insect biotypes and incorporating these
genes into cultivars.

A hazard of genetic uniformity that has not received as
much attention is the potential effect of genetic erosion on
the agronomic performance of future cultivars. It seems
inevitable that the continual recycling of a few elite
genotypes that trace back to narrow, and often commonly
derived, sources must lead eventually to a genetic ceiling
on crop improvement. There is no hard evidence that this
yet happened. Plant breeders continue to be successful in
meeting the varied and often changing needs of agriculture
(Sprague et al. 1980). Yield in several crops has increased
steadily, through breeding, at a rate of about 1% per year
(Evans 1980, Kannenberg 1981, Luedders 1977) and steady

---

[1]The southern corn leaf blight epidemic was not due to
genetic uniformity but rather the extensive use of a particular male-sterile cytoplasm.

progress continues to be made in selection for other desirable agronomic traits. This, however, doesn't mean that genetic variability is inexhaustible. The pedigree system of crop breeding, in which the best cultivars or lines of each generation are the parents for the next generation of cultivars or lines, has been intensively employed in most crops only within the last 50-60 years. The number of cycles of selection is in fact relatively small. Luedders (1977) states that effectively two cycles have been completed in 47 years of modern soybean breeding. Duvick (1977) indicates that present corn inbreds represent the third cycle of pedigree selections with about 13 years between cycles. Data from Eslick and Hockett (1974) show that there have been about 7 cycles of pedigree selection in malting barley since the early 1900's. The situation in the Canadian bread wheats is also similar.[1]

Reduction. In recent years, there has been increasing interest in breeding procedures that reduce the rate of genetic erosion inherent in the pedigree system. The shift away from the pedigree system has been most apparent in corn breeding, although the pedigree approach still dominates the industry. A survey by the American Seed Trade Association (ASTA) showed that in 1975 19% of new inbred line development was from synthetic populations, i.e., populations derived from intercrossing of selected components (usually several elite inbred lines), 15% of new line development was from exotic X adapted crosses, and 15% was from populations improved through cyclic recurrent selection (Zuber 1975).

The shift toward a population approach to corn breeding has been encouraged by two factors. The first is the impact on the hybrid corn industry of Iowa Stiff Stalk Synthetic (BSSS), a synthetic population developed in the late 1930s by intercrossing just 16 inbred lines and subsequently improved by cyclic recurrent selection. This relatively narrow-based population was in 1975 the source, directly or indirectly, of inbred lines used in about one-third of North American hybrid seed production (Zuber 1975). About 15 inbred lines from BSSS are used to a significant extent by the hybrid corn industry. Two of these, B73 and A632, were involved directly in nearly 30% of North American hybrid seed productions in 1979 (Zuber, personal communication[2]).

---

[1]Handbook of Canadian Varieties. The Searle Grain Company Limited. Winnipeg, Manitoba.

---

[2]Zuber, M.S. University of Missouri, Columiba, Missouri.

Thus, in 1980, some 10 million hectares of corn were planted to hybrids having one of these two inbred lines in their pedigree. This is an underestimate since it does not include lines derived from these two inbreds. The second factor encouraging the shift toward somewhat broader-based sources than used in traditional systems has been concern about the potential hazards associated with an ever-narrowing genetic base, a concern emphasized by the Southern corn leaf blight epidemic of 1970.

Cyclic recurrent selection, the method used to improve BSSS, is a breeding procedure designed to increase the frequency of favorable genes in a population while minimizing the loss of genetic variability. There are several different recurrent selection schemes (Sprague and Eberhart 1977, Gardner 1978), but the general procedure is to identify, often by progeny testing, several superior individuals in a population and then intercrossing them, or their immediate progeny, to form the next cycle. The procedure is then repeated on a continuing basis. The various recurrent selection schemes have been studied most comprehensively in corn. They have been shown to be effective, both in progressively improving successive cycles of the population and the inbred lines derived from each cycle (Sprague and Eberhart 1977, Gardner 1978).

The population approach to breeding slows down the rate of genetic erosion relative to the pedigree system as well as offering the opportunity for broadening the genetic base. This opportunity, however, has been taken only to a limited extent. This is best evidenced by the source materials used in corn population improvement programs at public institutions in the ten states that comprise most of the U.S. Corn Belt. A 1977 NCR-2 survey[1] of these institutions indicated that improvement programs were underway in a total of 246 populations. This suggests a broad sampling of corn germplasm, but such is not the case. Many of the populations have the same source or are constructed from similar, elite materials. For example, the 246 populations include 24 of BSSS, 20 from three open-pollinated Corn Belt varieties, and 133 synthetics formed from Corn Belt inbreds. Although 62 of the 246 populations were identified as containing at least some exotic germplasm, the proportion of exotic germplasm was often minimal. About 10 populations

---

[1]In: Report of the North Central Corn Breeding Research Committee (NCR-2) Meeting. 1977. Chicago, Illinois. pp 64-110. Reported by Arnel R. Hallauer Iowa State University.

were developed solely from exotic sources.   The exotic
materials and possibly some of the open-pollinated populations represent the only influx of new germplasm.   The
redundancy of germplasm exemplified by the above undoubtedly
reflects the general breeding philosophy of concentrating
effort on the best performing available germplasm.

It is of course not realistic to expect breeders to
discard proven materials and proven approaches because of
something that might happen in the future.   We know far too
little about the nature and magnitude of genetic variability,   even within so-called narrow base populations,   to
predict with certainty that we are well on our way to a
genetic ceiling on crop improvement.   However, there are
reasons why breeders should expend at least a portion of
their total effort on projects to broaden significantly the
genetic base of their breeding populations.   One reason is
simply as insurance against reaching a genetic ceiling.   It
is not sufficient to wait until there is clear evidence that
such a ceiling has been reached before seeking new genetic
resources.   Modern cultivars represent a very high level of
agronomic performance and considerable time will likely be
required before new breeding sources can be brought to a
point where they are competitive with materials from the
ongoing system.   This is assuming, of course, that the rate
of improvement in new, broader-based breeding sources will
be greater than in the present materials so that ultimately
the new sources will exceed the performance of the ongoing
materials.

Another, perhaps more compelling, reason for developing
new breeding sources has been suggested by Frankel (1977).
He points out that new sources may introduce alternative or
additional gene complexes which may result in new developmental pathways and ecological adaptation.   It seems
unlikely that the few original sources of most modern
cultivars would have embodied all the best developmental
pathways for agronomic productivity, especially considering
that screening of the original sources was basically for
adaptation and not performance under intensive cultural
practices.   If new sources do, in fact, have some alternative and perhaps better systems, both the rate of improvement and the genetic ceiling might be raised significantly.

An indirect benefit of broad-based populations would be
the increased genetic diversity among cultivars or lines
bred from them.   Even if breeders used broad-based
populations of similar origin, the population structure
would likely change from program to program.   The diversity

of cultivars or lines from such populations could be of
significant value as a defense against disease and insect
epidemics.

Sources of Diversity

What sources of diversity are available to the plant
breeder?   Sizeable collections can be found in germplasm
banks at various national, international and regional
centres.   The total number of accessions for various crops
are in the order of 30,000 for wheat (Harlan 1972), 50,000
for rice (Chang 1979), 16,000 for barley (Eslick and Hockett
1974), 35,000 for maize (Brown 1979; Lonnquist 1974), 22,000
for sorghum (Webster 1976), and 13,000 for soybeans (Bernard
1976, Kwan 1976, Kaizume 1976).   The United States Department of Agriculture maintains significant collections of
these and other crops.   The inadequacies of these collections and the urgent need to complete collections while wild
races and primitive cultivars are still extant have been
pointed out repeatedly (e.g. Timothy and Goodman 1979,
Frankel 1977, Frankel and Hawkes 1975, Frankel and Bennett
1970, Harlan 1972).   There can be no question of the neces-
sity of comprehensive, well-maintained collections that are
properly described and catalogued.   My point, however, is
that the plant breeder even now has access to a considerable
diversity of germplasm.   To date, this germplasm has been
used only in a limited way, primarily by systematic
screening of collections for genetic resistance to pests and
diseases (Frankel 1977), so that these genes can be incorporated into modern cultivars.   Indeed many breeders
consider the principal value of germplasm collections to be
simply as potential sources of hitherto unneeded genes for
disease and insect resistance.

Why haven't breeders used these collections to broaden
the genetic base of their breeding populations?   A major
problem is that in many crops most accessions are exotics,
i.e, germplasm which cannot be used directly in a breeding
program because of differential responses for such factors
as photoperiod, temperature, winter hardiness, vernaliza-
tion, etc.   The task of adaptation and acclimatization of
exotic germplasm typically requires a long-term and
sometimes complex program of selection and recombination
(Hallauer 1978, Webster 1976), although the use of crosses
between exotic and adapted genotypes can speed up the
process.   The effort required probably dictates that only
very elite exotic materials can be considered for eventual
incorportion into breeding populations.   Of course,
collections that are exotic to one area are adapted to
another.   Ultimately, exchange of elite breeding stocks

among breeders in different parts of the world could lead to considerable introgression of exotic materials. Breeding programs at the various international crop improvement centres are important sources of such materials.

However, many accessions are reasonably adapted. Their major drawback is that they are often very unsatisfactory by present day agronomic standards. Accessions of this category would include primitive cultivars or land races. These accessions, however, could have favorable genes or gene complexes that are over-shadowed by their undesirable traits. After all, our modern cultivars originated from such sources. The few programs that incorporate accessions generally will not use an accession or an introduction, e.g., material from another breeder, unless it at least approaches the performance of the ongoing materials. The reasoning is that such materials, even though it may contain some favorable genes, will result in a general dilution of the standards of the breeding population and therefore lessen the probability of extracting superior cultivars or lines. The net result is that the "new" germplasm introduced into most breeding programs is, most frequently, advanced cultivars from other breeding programs and is often of similar background (Frankel 1977). These advanced materials are, of course, valuable and have a major role to play in all breeding programs, but they do not represent significant advances in genetic diversity.

New Breeding Approaches

There has been in recent years an awakening interest in breeding approaches which have one or more of the following objectives:

1) a significant broadening of the genetic base deployed in breeding programs,
2) a reduction in the rate of genetic erosion by employing a population approach to breeding, and
3) an increase in favorable gene frequencies, with minimal loss of genetic variability, through cyclic recurrent selection.

In many cross fertilized crops, breeders have traditionally used some form of recurrent selection in cultivar development. A few breeders of self-pollinated crops also are now using this procedure, especially when male-sterility can be used to facilitate recombinations.

Examples of programs with the above objectives follow. Some of these are at the proposal stage; others have been activated. Hanson, et al. (1972) have proposed a co-operative scheme whereby worldwide collections of alfalfa germplasm would be deployed to seven regional locations in the United States, based on such factors as origin, photoperiodic response, cold tolerance, pest resistance, etc. Within each region, these would be intercrossed with domestic stocks and the resulting gene pool subjected to mild mass selection to provide improved source material for breeding regionally adapted, multiple pest-resistant varieties. This program, in a modified form, is now in the very early stages of its development (Barnes 1980).

In sorghum, a co-operative breeding program has been developed to transfer germplasm from tropical cultivars into semi-dwarf, day-neutral genotypes that can be used directly to broaden the genetic base of breeding programs (Webster 1976). Some sorghum programs are using male sterility to incorporate such germplasm into breeding populations. In the small grains, several systems are being employed to increase useable genetic variability. Jensen (1970) has developed a diallel selective mating system which embodies the concepts of broad working gene pools, selective matings, and mass and recurrent selection.

Ramage (1978) employs male-sterility to facilitate cyclical recurrent selections in broad-based barley populations. This program is in many respects an extension of the evolutionary breeding approach of Suneson and Wiebe (1962) although the latter relied on natural selection. Moseman (1976) has developed a procedure which utilizes genetic male sterility for breeding disease resistant barley cultivars with diverse genetic bases.

A co-operative program between Oregon State University and The International Maize and Wheat Improvement Center (CIMMYT) has been developed to broaden the genetic base of wheat by systematically crossing winter and spring germplasm (Kern 1980). Advanced lines are distributed to co-operators for international testing and selected lines are reincorporated into the system.

In soybeans, co-operative regional yield evaluations are being employed to identify productive plant introductions. Kenworthy (1980) has proposed a system to incorporate such introductions into base breeding populations which are then improved through cyclical recurrent selection.

As part of my corn breeding program at the University of Guelph, I have initiated a hierarchical, open-ended system (HOPE). This system is described in detail elsewhere (Kannenberg 1981), but a brief description of the aims and procedures follows.

HOPE

Hierarchical Open Ended System. HOPE is designed both to broaden significantly the genetic base of breeding populations and to provide an improved source for the development of inbred lines that are useful to a hybrid-oriented technology. In a traditional population improvement program these objectives tend to be mutually exclusive, i.e., the broader the genetic base, the poorer the agronomic performance of the population, and the lower the probability of obtaining useful cultivars or inbred lines. For this reason, breeders typically require that introductions into their programs meet certain minimum standards of performance. Thus, germplasm is discarded in which the effects of unfavorable genes mask or override those of favorable genes. As indicated earlier, this would include most exotic germplasm and primitive cultivars. The HOPE system, however, is designed to allow incorporation of the full array of germplasm available to the breeder. HOPE does this by establishing a hierarchy of successively better performing populations to include low, intermediate, high, and elite levels. Initially, 6-8 components, to include open-pollinated varieties, composites, and synthetics, were assigned, based on performance testing, to each gene pool of the hierarchy except the elite level. The components for a given gene pool were systematically and repeatedly intercrossed to form each initial population. The elite level gene pools were established later from selections of the high performance gene pools. The hierarchical approach separates material with poor agronomic characteristics on average from immediately more useful germplasm. The system, however, does allow for the eventual introgression of desirable genes and gene complexes into the elite populations. It accomplishes that by being open-ended in the sense that material can be move progressively through the hierarchy.

In a hybrid-oriented crop, such as corn, it is essential to produce inbred lines that have good combining ability. To accomplish this, the HOPE system utilizes two complementary gene pools, an "A" and a "B" pool, at each level of the hierarchy. Thus, a total of eight gene pools are employed. Essentially, the germplsm in the four hierarchical populations of the "A" series is complementary to the germplasm of the "B" series. Thus inbred lines derived from the Elite "A" population should on average produce hybrids with good vigor when crossed with inbred lines from the Elite "B" population.   Inbred lines are developed only from the two elite populations.

A broad-based breeding system must be able to accom-modate additional germplasm as it becomes available to the breeder. In traditional population breeding, introductions are rarely incorporated in the ongoing system.   They are either put "on the shelf" for potential future use or, if the breeder's resources permit, another population is initiated. There are two undesirable aspects of this. The first is that valuable germplasm may never be used. For example, the 1977 NCR-2 survey (ibid) indicated that an additional 200 populations were available but were not being worked on. The second is that the breeder may soon find that the number of populations he is working with has proliferated beyond his ability to maintain effective control over them. The HOPE system, as are most of the modern breeding systems noted earlier, is open-ended in that new germplasm can be added at any time. An introduction is first tested for its per se performance in order to estab-lish its appropriate level in the hierarchy, except that no introduction is assigned directly to the elite level. Then, the introduction is topcrossed to each elite population and the topcross is evaluated to determine whether the introduction belongs to the "A" or "B" heterotic pattern. Material which does not have a clear "A" or "B" pattern is assigned to either at random. Introductions per se are not added directly to the appropriate gene pool, but rather the topcross of the introduction to the elite gene pool is used as an entry. This serves two purposes. First, the overall "A" and "B" heterotic pattern is reinforced and, second, the ongoing gene pools are not overwhelmed by an influx of new germplasm. For example, 365 introductions have been incor-rated in the last two years, about 90% into the low perform-ance gene pools.

The HOPE system utilizes increasingly stringent selec-tion procedures at each successive level of the hierarchy. The procedures employed include the grid system of mass selection (Gardner 1961) for the low performance popula-tions, modified ear-to-row selection (Lonnquist 1964) for the intermediate and high performance populations, and reciprocal recurrent selections with an inbred tester (Russell and Eberhart 1975) for the elite populations.   A very general description of these procedures follows. Mass selection, a procedure in which selection is based on the appearance of individual open-pollinated plants, is used at the low performance level because this procedure maximizes genetic   recombination   and   maintenance   of   genetic variability. Most new material enters the system at this level and the opportunity for maximum recombination and minimal genetic loss is particularly important because of this. The modified ear-to-row procedure, which is used at the intermediate and high performance levels of the hierarchy, requires progeny testing of open-pollinated selections. Variability is maintained because of open-pollination, but progeny testing allows more effective identification of superior entries. A higher selection intensity is employed at the high level than at the intermediate level, i.e., fewer entries are chosen in the high performance population than in the intermediate performance pool for recombining to form the next cycle. This should result in a faster rate of improvement in the high performance populations compared to the intermediate populations and should also enhance the likelihood of superior progenies for advancement to the elite level. The reciprocal recurrent selection procedure, as I employ it at the elite level, involves the selection of a very few entries which are chosen primarily on the basis of their performance in crosses with an inbred line derived from the other elite population. The selections are also screened for their resistance to certain diseases and the European corn borer. Plants of the second selfed (S_2) generation of the selected entries are intercrossed to form the next cycle. The emphasis on combining ability with the opposite population is in order to increase the probability of extracting good combining inbred lines from the elite populations. Inbreds are developed from each cycle by continuing the selfing of the S_2 selections chosen to form the next cycle of the elite populations.

The movement of genes through the system is accomplished as follows. The six best entries from the high performance population are interplanted systematically in the low performance, mass selection block and are detassled prior to pollen shed. The bulked, open-pollinated seed from each of the six entries is then used as an entry in the next cycle of the intermediate performance gene pool. This procedure not only allows introgression of genes from the low performance gene pool into the intermediate performance gene pool but the use of the high performance entries as the gene carriers also helps to reenforce the overall "A" and "B" heterotic pattern. Entries in the intermediate performance gene pool that exceed the average performance of the high performance gene pool are used as entries in the next cycle of the high performance population. However, these entries are also maintained in the intermediate performance population in order to maintain the overall performance level of this population. Thus, the selected entries essentially act as bridges to move genes between the two gene pools. Entries that are not selected for the next cycle of the intermediate or high performance gene pools are not discarded. Instead, they are incorporated into the low performance gene pool because, on average, these materials should be better than the materials in the low performance pool. The initial cycle of the elite populations was formed from selections out of the three best entries of the high performance gene pools. Subsequently, new entries from the high performance gene pool will only be incorporated into the elite population if they exceed the performance of the ongoing elite materials. Although the elite populations have a very restricted genetic base and are being subjected to very stringent selection, genetic variability should not be a problem because there is the potential for the addition of new germplasm in every cycle.

To date, only germplasm early enough to mature under the short-season conditions at Guelph has been used in the HOPE system. Most introductions are open-pollinated varieties, synthetics, or composites received from other breeders of short-season corn or from the North Central Regional Plant Introductions Station at Ames, Iowa. A few HOPE components include longer-season germplasm, usually in the form of recurrently selected materials from exotic X adapted crosses. A program has been initiated to use a few elite sources of long-season, even tropical, germplasm. This program will require several years of crossing and selection before the material will be of suitable maturity for incorporation into the HOPE system.

In summary, the main features of the HOPE system are:

1)   HOPE is hierarchical. Structuring of the germplasm into different performance levels permits the use of a broad array of germplasm, but separates the germplasm of more immediate value from germplasm in which desirable genes may be masked or overshadowed by agronomically undesirable characteristics.

2)   HOPE is open-ended. New germplasm can be added continually to the system and genes and gene complexes from ongoing materials can be moved progressively through the hierarchy. The continual influx and flow of germplasm throughout the system ensure the maintenance of extensive genetic variability even at the high and elite performance levels.

3)   HOPE employs progressively stringent selection

procedures. The mass selection procedure used at the low performance level maximizes genetic recombination and minimizes genetic loss. The procedures employed at the intermediate and high level are designed to be increasingly more selective of desirable genotypes but also to conserve genetic variability. At the elite performance level, the populations are formed from a few of the best selections of the high performance gene pools and the populations are exposed to very intensive selection. Erosion of genetic variability at the elite performance level is not considered important because of the open-ended concept.

4)   HOPE is based on a heterotic pattern. This is an essential feature in a hybrid-oriented crop. Although the heterotic pattern is determined at the elite performance level, the system is structured to reenforce the "A" and "B" pattern at each peformance level.

Thus, the overall intent of the HOPE design is to maximize genetic diversity and to shape this diversity into a form which can be used to produce a continuing series of genetically dissimilar inbred lines that exhibit good combining ability in hybrid combination. It is too early in the program to determine whether HOPE will be successful and, if so, how soon useful inbreds will be produced. Selection has been underway since 1977, but the first cycle of the elite populations was formed in the 1979-80 winter nursery. The first inbred lines produced will be from the components used to form the initial cycle of the elite populations. These will be ready for testing in 1983 and inbreds from the first and subsequent cycles will be produced at two-year intervals thereafter.

Conclusion

I believe that it is imperative that measures be taken to broaden the working base of crop species, particularly in the agriculturally developed countries where the breeding methods employed have eroded the genetic base. It is not sufficient to rely on latent genetic variability in gene banks. This variability should be activated and deployed now to ensure the continued development of crop cultivars with steadily increasing performance. In some crop species, the present day standards may be such that the time required to bring broad-based material to a competitive level would be prohibitive for an individual breeder. For example, this could be the case in the Canadian bread wheats because of the quality standards. In these instances, it is the responsibility of government agricultural agencies to ensure that germplasm improvement work is initiated and that breeders working in this area receive adequate support and recognition.

Literature Cited

Barnes, D.K. 1980. Status of alfalfa germplasm collection, preservation, maintenance, and utilization in 1980. Report to the National Plant Genetics Resources Board 6-10-80.

Bernard, R.L. 1976. United States national germplasm collection. In: L.D. Hill, ed., World Soybean Research, The Interstate Printers & Publishers, Inc., Danville, Illinois. pp. 286-289.

Brown, W.L. 1979. Development and improvement of the germplasm base of modern maize. Proceedings IX Meeting Eucarpia Corn and Sorghum Sect. pp. 93-111.

Chang, T.T. 1979. Crop genetic resources. In: J. Sneep and A.J.T. Hendriksen, eds., Plant breeding perspectives, Centre for Agricultural Publishing and Documentation, Wageningen. pp. 83-103.

Committee on Genetic Vulnerability of Major Crops. 1972. Genetic vulnerability of major crops. Nat. Acad. Sci., Washington, D.C.

Duvick, D.N. 1977. Major United States crops in 1976. Ann. N.Y. Acad. Sci. 287: 86-96.

Eslick, R.F., and E.A. Hockett. 1974. Genetic engineering as a key to water-use efficiency. Agric. Meteorol. 13-23.

Evans, L.T. 1980. The natural history of crop yield. Amer. Sci. 68: 388-397.

Frankel, O.H. 1977. Genetic resources. Ann. N.Y. Acad. Sci. 287: 332-344.

_____, and E. Bennett, eds. 1970. Genetic resources in plants – their exploration and conservation. IBP Handbook No. 11, Blackwell Scientific Publications, Oxford, England.

_____, and J.G. Hawkes, eds. 1975. Crop genetic resources for today and tomorrow. Cambridge Univ. Press, Cambridge, England.

Gardner, C.O. 1961. An evaluation of effects of mass selection and seed irradiation with thermal neutrons on yield of corn. Crop Sci. 1: 241-245.

_____. 1978. Population improvement in maize. In: D.B. Walden, ed., Maize breeding and genetics, John Wiley and Sons, New York. pp. 207-228.

Goodman, M.M., and R. McK.Bird. 1977. The races of maize IV: Tentative grouping of 219 Latin American Races. Econ. Bot. 31: 204-221.

Hallauer, A.R. 1978. Potential of exotic germplasm for maize improvement. In: D.B. Walden, ed., Maize breeding and genetics, John Wiley and Sons, New York. pp. 229-247.

Hanson, C.H., T.H. Busbice, R.R. Hill, Jr., O.J. Hunt, and A.J. Oakes. 1972. Directed mass selection for developing multiple pest resistance and conserving germplasm in alfalfa. J. Environ. Qual. 1: 106-111.

Harlan, J.R. 1972. Genetics of disaster. J. Environ. Qual. 1: 212-215.

Hartwig, E.E. 1973. Varietal development. In: B.C. Caldwell, ed., Soybeans: improvement, production, and uses, American Society of Agronomy, Madison, Wisc. pp. 187-210.

Jensen, N.F. 1970. A diallel selective mating system for cereal breeding. Crop Sci. 10: 629-635.

Kaizuma, N. 1976. Japanese germplasm collection. In: L.D. Hill, ed., World soybean research, The Interstate Priners & Publishers, Inc., Danville, Illinois. pp. 298-305.

Kannenberg, L.W. 1981. Activation and deployment of genetic resources in a maize breeding program. In: G.G.E. Seudder and J.L. Reveal, eds., Evolution Today. Proceedings of Second Internat. Congr. of System. and Evoln. Biol., Univ. Brit. Col., Vancouver, B.C. pp. 392-399.

Kenworthy, W.J. 1980. Strategies for introgressing exotic germplasm in breeding programs. In: F.T. Corbin, ed., World soybean research conference II: Proceedings. Westview Press, Boulder, Colorado. pp. 217-223.

Kern, K. Robert. 1980. Probing the gene pools - spring x winter crosses in bread wheat. CIMMYT TODAY No. 12. Centro Internacional de Mejoramiento de Maiz y Trigo. 11 pp.

Kwan, S.H. 1976. Korean germplasm collection. In: L.D. Hill, ed., World soybean research, The Interstate Printers & Publishers, Inc., Danville, Illinois. pp. 290-297.

Lonnquist, J.H. 1964. A modification of the ear-to-row procedure for the improvement of maize populations. Crop Sci. 4: 227-228.

_____. 1974. Conservation and experiences with recombinations of exotic and Corn Belt maize germplasm. Proc. Twenty-ninth Ann. Corn and Sorghum Research Conf. 29: 102-117.

Luedders. V.D. 1977. Genetic improvement in yield of soybeans. Crop Sci. 17: 971-972.

Marshall, D.R. 1977. The advantages and hazards of genetic homogeneity. Ann N.Y. Acad. Sci. 287: 1-20.

Moseman, J.G. 1976. Controlled facilitated recurrent selection of barley. Amer. Soc. of Agron. Abstr. p. 57.

Ramage, R.R. 1978. Male sterile facilitated recurrent selection. Barley Newsletter 22: 56-59.

Russell, W.A., and S.A. Eberhart. 1975. Hybrid performance of selected maize lines from reciprocal recurrent and testcross selection programs. Crop Sci. 15: 1-4.

Sprague, G.F., and D.E. Alexander, and J.W. Dudley. 1980. Plant breeding and genetic engineering: a perspective. BioSci. 30: 17-21.

Sprague, G.F., and S.A. Eberhart. 1977. Corn breeding. In: G.F. Sprague, ed., Corn and corn improvement, American Society of Agronomy, Madison, Wisc. pp. 305-362.

Suneson, C.A. and G.A. Wiebe. 1962. A "Paul Bunyan" plant breeding enterprise with barley. Crop Sci. 2: 347-348.

Taylor, N.L., P.B. Gibson, and W.E. Knight. 1977. Genetic vulnerability and germplasm resources of the true clovers. Crop Sci. 17: 632-634.

Timothy, D.H., and M.M. Goodman. 1979. Germplasm preservation: The basis of future feast or famine genetic
resources of maize -- an example. In: I. Rubenstein,
R.L. Phillips, C.E. Green, and B.G. Gengenbach, eds., The
plant seed: development, preservation, and germination,
Academic Press, Inc., New York. pp. 171-200.

Webster, O.J. 1976. Sorghum vulnerability and germplasm
resources. Crop Sci. 16: 553-556.

Zuber, M.S. 1975. Corn germplasm base in the U.S. - is it
narrowing, widening, or static? Proceedings Thirtieth
Ann. Corn and Sorghum Research Conf. 30: 277-286.

10. Gene Centers and Gene Utilization in American Agriculture

Introduction

American agriculture is an imported agriculture. With the exception of corn (maize), all of the important crops were introduced to the country after European contact. The early settlers brought seeds with them. They sent home to relatives for more. Governors, consuls, ambassadors, and travellers in foreign parts were always alert to additional sources. Seeds and planting stock came in a stream through both private and governmental efforts. Yet, the pattern was set early on; a handful of sources for each crop provided the germ plasm that laid the foundations of American agriculture. Only a tiny fraction of the introductions had the adaptation required. By the early decades of this century, American plant germ plasm was so superior in performance that new and exotic introductions had little chance of success on their own. They could be useful as sources of specific characters for improvement of adapted cultivars, but the basic foundations had been set.

Where did our germ plasm _really_ come from? What relationships, if any, did it have to gene centers? I shall attempt to sketch the basic sources that built agriculture in the U.S., then comment on current trends in gene utilization. As a sample of crops, I have selected the 15 most valuable as listed for 1978 in the U.S. Department of Agriculture's "Agricultural Statistics 1979" (Table 1). The figure given for "farm value" is used for each crop except alfalfa, for which no value is estimated. Calculations for farm value of alfalfa are indicated under the discussion of that crop.

It is difficult to establish a time when the basic germplasm had jelled because it varied from crop to crop but

Table 1.   Most Valuable Crop Awards, 1978

	Crop	(U.S. $ Billions)
1.	Corn	14.9
2.	Soybean	12.2
3.	Alfalfa	5.3 +
4.	Wheat	5.3 -
5.	Cotton	3.1
6.	Tobacco	2.7
7.	Sorghum	1.4
8.	Potatoes	1.3
9.	Oranges	1.2
10.	Rice	1.1
11.	Tomatoes	0.8
12.	Peanuts	0.8
13.	Barley	0.8
14.	Oats	0.7
15.	Sugarbeets	0.6

From USDA Agricultural Statistics 1979.

World War II may be used as something of a watershed. Although some of our current trends in germ plasm utilization and exploitation were foreshadowed before that time, there is a sufficient difference that it is convenient to treat the evolution of our crops before and after this event.   During the settling of our country and up until World War II, the basic sources of germ plasm were introduced and stabilized.   Emphasis was on adaptation.   If plant explorers were sent out, they were sent to regions with a climate similar to or a little more extreme than those for which material was needed.   Relatively little attention was paid to gene centers as such.   They were not altogether ignored; H.V. Harlan explored Ethiopia before Vavilov, and G.N. Collins, J.H. Kempton, Mark Carleton, David Fairchild, and others were collecting in gene centers long before the term was coined. But the most successful stocks generally came from regions resembling those in which the crop is grown in the U.S.

Before World War II

1.   Corn.   The farm value of corn shown in table 1 is underestimated.   It does not include corn for silage or fodder, popcorn, sweet corn,   or seed corn, and the latter is a very large industry.   The commercial corns of the U.S.

were generated <u>in situ</u> from a combination of so-called northern flints and southern dents. The northern flints would be more properly called eastern flints since they have been found archaeologically from Canada to Texas, Alabama, and Georgia. They were the dominant corns east of the Mississippi. There were a few incursions into Illinois and Ohio of types found in the Great Plains and the Southwest and the gourdseed dents were grown on a small scale from Chesapeake Bay southwards. The flints go back at least a thousand years in eastern U.S., but there is no evidence of early gourdseed dents. Ultimate provenance can only be speculative, but the recently introduced dents probably came from Mexico and the flints most nearly resemble those of the highlands of Guatemala; they do not appear to be Mexican (Anderson and Brown 1952).

Wallace and Brown (1956) describe in some detail how Robert Reid accidentally produced hybrids between the two races. He moved from near Cincinnati to a farm near Peoria, Illinois, taking with him a favorite variety of southern dent obtained from one Gordon Hopkins and tracing to Rockingham County, Virginia. His first crop in Illinois in 1846 did not mature well, and as a result, he got a poor stand in 1847. He replanted the missing hills in June with an early flint. From the hybrid offspring he and his son, James, selected Reid's yellow Dent over a period of years. This and related selections became one of the main breeding families of corn belt corn. Many useful inbreds have been selected from it, and the variety was incorporated with other similar sources into the stiff-stalk synthetic which has, perhaps, contributed more usable inbreds than any other gene pool. "Accidents" of this type happened all over the corn-growing sections of the U.S. Another source that has contributed enormously to the corn belt was a gene pool based on Lancaster Surecrop and related strains.

2. <u>Soybean</u>. Sources of U.S. soybean germ plasm are given in detail by Hartwig (1973). The main strains trace to introductions from Manchuria in 1911 which yielded Lincoln and its derivatives, and in 1926 which yielded Richland and its derivatives. The cultivars in use in the northern and north central states are almost entirely derived from these sources. There is a somewhat wider genetic base in southern cultivars where a source from Korea, one from Japan, and material from Nanking have been used. Soybean is one of the few of our important crops for which we have made direct use of accessions derived from what may be a center of origin. It will be noted, however, that the climate and latitude of Manchuria are very similar to that of the northern soybean

growing area.   More southern sources were used to improve adaptation for the South.

3.   <u>Alfalfa</u>. Statistics for alfalfa are quaintly hidden in a chapter entitled "Statistics for hay, seeds, and minor field crops" (USDA 1979). They inform us that 86.7 million tons of alfalfa are produced in 1978, but no value is estimated. A rather meaningless figure of $50.00 per ton is given for "all hay." Obviously, alfalfa hay is worth more than grass and wild hay. Prices by states ranged from $28 to $75 per ton, according to the data given. I therefore used the figure of $60 per ton x 86.7 million tons or 5.2 billion as the value of the hay crop. To this may be added the farm value of alfalfa seed, indicated as 0.1 billion since alfalfa seed production is a separate industry. The rounded figure of 5.3 billion is probably conservative and does not include mixed sowings for grazing.

There were early and sporadic introductions of alfalfa in colonial times, but the crop had little success until seed from Chile was introduced into California in about 1850 in connection with the gold rush. This material was the major source of the commons known by the state of origin. Kansas and Oklahoma commons were sufficiently winter hardy for parts of Illinois, Ohio, and Pennsylvania; Arizona and Texas commons, generally, were not.   None had adequate hardiness for the northern states. Good sources of winter hardiness were derived from Grimm, introduced from Germany by Wendeline Grimm in 1858 and by Baltic from northern Europe in 1896, Cossack from Russia in 1907, and Ladak from the Himalayas of Kashmir in 1910.   Turkestan, introduced from central Asia in 1898 has contributed much in the way of disease and insect resistance as well as drought tolerance and general hardiness (Bolton et al. 1972).

For the U.S. southwest, where winter hardiness is not a problem, more productive types from Peru, India, and Egypt have been obtained (Hanson and Davis 1972). Finally, the Flamande types from France have been useful in providing short-rotation, high-yielding types, although they arrived shortly after World War II.   In a sample of current cultivars in use we may trace origins as follows:

Chile: commons, Buffalo, Cody, Caliverde,
                Williamsburg.
Central Asia: Cossack, Ladak, Turkestan, and Ranger
                derived from these.
Turkestan: Namastan, Orestan, Lohontan, Washoe,
                Hardistan.

Egypt: Moapa, Sonora.
India: Sirsa.
France: DuPuits, Saranac, Apex, Stride, Thor,
                Anchor, Apalachee.

The Turkestan, Cossack, and Ladak introductions are the
only ones that might be considered to relate more or less
directly to a center or origin, and these are specialized
and derived, compared to the wild races of the region.

4. Wheat. The farm value figure shown for wheat does not
include value as grazing, which might be sufficient to
displace alfalfa as the number three crop in farm value.

More striking than the growth of an oak from an acorn
is the fact that the vast hard red spring wheat
industry in the United States, with all the milling,
baking, transportation, and trading dependent on it,
developed from a few seeds saved from a single wheat
plant.

So wrote J.A. Clark (1936) in describing the origin of
Marquis, which he considered "the greatest achievement in
wheat-breeding history." Actually, this wasn't quite the
whole story. The source could be traced from Galicia in
Poland to Germany to Scotland to Canada, where a single
plant selection by David Fife of Ontario produced Red Fife.
It was C.E. Saunders, also of Canada, who crossed Red Fife
and Hard Red Calcutta from India and selected Marquis, later
to be a parent of Ceres, Hope, Reward, Marquillo, Reliance,
Thatcher, Sturgeon, Comet, and Temmarq, among others. Red
Fife was introduced into the U.S. about 1860 and Marquis in
1912. Marquis soon set the standard for all hard red spring
wheats, and is used today as the genetic stock into which
rust resistance genes are inserted as standard differentials
for the identification of races of rust.

But, Marquis was no more remarkable than Turkey,
introduced into Kansas by Mennonite immigrants from Russia
about 1873. The first reliable variety survey was made in
1919 and revealed that Turkey occupied 99% of the hard red
winter wheat area and constituted 30% of the total U.S.
wheat acreage. It was seeded on over 21 million acres,
almost twice that of any other cultivar at the time. It was
highly variable, and numerous lines have been selected from
it, hybridized, and selected again. The hard red winter
wheat industry traces largely to this source today.
Furthermore, Turkey was one of the parents of Norin 10, the
source of the semi-dwarfing genes used in modern wheats
around the world. The Japanese had obtained Turkey from the

U.S. in 1892 and used it in the development of some of their wheats, including Norin 10 (Quisenberry and Reitz 1974).

The soft wheat belt of the eastern states was also dominated by a single heterogeneous source, although not quite so completely. The source was called Mediterranean when it was introduced in 1819, probably from Italy. It was transformed by repeated selections to Lancaster to Fultz (1862), Fulcaster (1886), Leap (1906), Trumbull (1916), Fulhio (1918), and others.

The western white wheat industry was early dominated by two introductions from Australia, Baart introduced in 1900, and Federation introduced in 1914. Federation was bred by William Farrer of New South Wales, but the germ plasm was no stranger to the U.S. The cultivar was selected from the cross Purplestraw x Yandilla. Purplestraw, source unknown, dates from 1822 in the U.S.; Yandilla was selected by Farrer from Red Fife x Etewah from India. The Indian material was used to introduce more heat tolerance for Australian conditions and this also fit the western states. Federation was,however, a sort of reconstruction of Marquis using a different Indian source.

The durum wheat belt was heavily influenced by Kubanka introduced from Russia by M.A. Carleton in 1901. Again, we see only the most remote and indirect relationship between U.S. germ plasm and anything like a center of origin. Far more important was _adaptation_. This was what, in fact, took Carleton to Russia and central Asia. As the wheat belt reached the high plains near the turn of the century, hardier types resistant to both cold and drought were needed.

5.   Cotton. The farm value indicated includes both lint (3.1 billion) and cotton-seed (0.2 billion).

Among long-staple cottons (_Gossypium barbadense_), Sea-Island was introduced to Georgia from the Bahama Islands in 1785, and Pima derived from a single plant selection out of material from Egypt in 1910. The history of upland cottons (_G. hirsutum_) is more complex, although the germ plasm, in general, came from Mexico. Many unrecorded and early introductions were made, and there is evidence for considerable importation of seeds after the Mexican War. A type called Mexican was brought to Natchez, Mississippi from Mexico City in 1806 and introduced to South Carolina about 1816. It was considered to be the stock from which most short and medium staple varieties were developed. Other important stocks were Texas Big Boll and Jackson Round Boll, the latter selected by James Jackson of Preston, Texas in the 1880's. Lone Star is a derivative, and has had considerable influence in cotton-growing countries of the world. Lone Star has, in turn, been the source of Lankart and Stoneville types important in the U.S.

Around the turn of the century, the boll weevil forced a move toward earlier, shorter staple types in an attempt to evade the worst effects of the pest. At the St. Louis Exposition of 1904, the Mexican Government displayed cotton from Durango which was soon to be the most popular cultivar under irrigation in Texas. In the winter of 1906-07, G.N. Collins and C.B. Doyle collected Acala and Tuxtla in southern Mexico. Acala types generally set the standard for upland cotton after that (Ware 1936).

6.   Tobacco.   Tobacco of sorts (<u>Nicotiana rustica</u>) was grown by the American Indians when the first colonists arrived. A small scale venture was begun by John Rolfe at Jamestown in 1612 with rustica material. This quickly gave way to <u>N. tabacum</u>. An early variety called Orinoco and probably derived from that region of South America, gave rise to the Virginia types. The other dominant stock was called Maryland Broadleaf, the source unknown but possibly derived from the West Indies. As settlers moved westward, they selected their own preferred types which eventually gave rise to the Burley tobaccos derived for the most part from Maryland Broadleaf. White Burley is a chlorotic mutant selected in 1864. About 1870, an introduction was obtained form Cuba that had considerable influence under the names Havana Seed, Connecticut Havana, Zimmer Spanish, Comstock Spanish, and so on. An introduction from Sumatra was used in breeding programs especially for cigar wrapper leaf, but was not grown much commercially. Other imports were rather minor. Maryland Mammoth was a short-day mutant that led to the discovery of photoperiod by Garner and Allard (Garner et al. 1936).

7.   Sorghum. The farm value for sorghum applies to grain only, and types grown for forage, silage, syrup, or broomcorn are not included. The sweet canes trace largely to two sources: Chinese Amber sent to France from the island of Tsungning in 1851 and thence to the U.S. in 1853, and a set of 16 accessions from Natal sent to Europe in 1854 by Leonard Wray and thence to the U.S. in 1857. Derivatives of these sources included Orange Sourless, Honey, Sumac, Gooseneck, White African, and the like. Another lot from Natal arrived via England in 1881 and contributed Collier.

The foundations of the grain sorghum industry were laid primarily by some white and brown durras introduced from Egypt to California in 1874, white and red kafirs from Natal, shown at the Centennial Exposition, Philadelphia 1876, milo which appeared in South Carolina about 1885, pink kafir from South Africa, 1904, and two important caudatum types from the Sudan, feterita (1960) and hegari (1908). There were many other introductions, but these stocks provided the bulk of the germ plasm. They were variable to begin with, but also seemed to mutate into more useful forms. Dwarfs and double dwarfs appeared. Hybridization and selection soon led to an array of cultivars better suited to the Great Plains than the original stocks. The locally derived sorts were so superior in adaptation that new introductions could not compete with them (Ball 1910, Martin 1936).

8.   Potatoes.   The early introductions of potato into the U.S. appear to be very obscure. There is a report that it was grown at Londonderry N.H. in 1719 from stock brought from Ireland, but there were probably earlier unrecorded importations. It was not until the second half of the 19th century that much activity in potato improvement is recorded. It is likely that selection and importation of European stocks was stimulated by the potato famines in Ireland during the late 1840's. One very influential stock was Goodrich's Garnet Chili selected by C.E. Goodrich, a clergyman, from imported Rough Purple Chili. Some 170 or so cultivars trace their ancestry to this selection, including important pre-Wrold War II commercial types such as Beauty of Hebron, Burbank, Early Ohio, Early Rose, Green Mountain, Prolific, and Triumph (Stevenson and Clark 1937).

9.   Oranges.   As of 1937, the California sweet orange industry was based on the Washington Navel and Valencia cultivars. The first was imported from the Bahia region of Brazil in 1870, the latter was distributed to both Florida and California by the English nurseryman Thomas Rivers in the 1870's. He obtained his stock from the Azores. The two varieties made year-long harvesting possible, since the Valencia is very late. The Valencia was named by A. Chapman of San Gabriel, California, following the suggestion of a Spanish laborer.

In Florida, October to May shipping was possible through the use of two early varieties, two midseason varieties, midseason seedlings, and the late Valencia. The principal named varieties were all from seedling sources selected in Florida orange groves. The early ones were Hamlin (1879) and Parson Brown (1878) and the midseason varieties were Pineapple and Homosassa selected in the 1870s (Traub and Robinson 1937).

10. Rice. The first rice of record in U.S. was grown in 1647 in Virginia from seed obtained from England by Governor Sir William Berkeley. According to M.A. Carleton (1920), the South Carolina industry began in 1694 when Governor Thomas Smith obtained a small bag from the captain of a ship which had taken shelter from storm in Charleston harbor. Jones (1936) suggested the seed came from Madagascar. Cultivars Carolina White and Carolina Gold were selected and served the region for 200 years. The Honduras variety was obtained from Honduras in 1890 and soon became the leading cultivar on the prairies of Louisiana, Texas, and Arkansas. It was a long-grained indica type. Most of the other significant introductions came from Japan. Of these, Early Wataribune introduced in 1913 was especially important as a source of Coloro, for about 50 years the leading rice variety in California. Blue Rose, selected in 1907 out of a field of Japanese rice in Louisiana, had a considerable influence not only in the U.S. but in some other rice-growing countries. Rexoro should also be mentioned as an important long-grained type derived from Marong-paroc introduced from the Philippines in 1911. Today California rice traces to Japan; Arkansas, Texas, and Louisiana rices tend toward Japonica-Indica derivatives.

11. Tomatoes. According to Boswell (1937), no tomato varieties had been developed in the United States before 1865. "The few varieties known had been brought in chiefly from England and a few from France. It appears that most of the large fruited varieties, if not all of them, had been obtained by selection from the old Large Red or ribbed type that had been known since about 1550." The first American cultivar was Tilden, selected by Henry Tilden of Davenport, Iowa in 1865. Trophy was selected by Dr. Hand of Baltimore County, Maryland in 1870, and contributed to most cultivars for the next 25 years. A.W. Livingston of Columbus, Ohio and later the Livingston Seed Company, contributed more to tomato selection than any other private group. Among many named varieties produced, Stone, released in 1899, is note-worthy because it in turn yielded Earliana selected by George Sparkes in 1900, and was one parent of Globe, introduced in 1905. The other parent of Globe was Ponderosa, selected by Peter Henderson in 1891. Marvel was selected by F.J. Pritchard of the USDA out of an introduction from France called Merveille des Marchée. Pritchard then crossed Marvel and Globe and selected out Marglobe, introduced in 1925. As Boswell put it in 1937, "Marglobe is without doubt the most important variety of

tomato in the United States and the world today." At that time it was the basis of the tomato industry in Florida, Mexico, Australia, and elsewhere. It is used today as a standard background for genetic stocks. It is thought by some (Jenkins 1948) that the tomato was domesticated in Mexico, but the commerical tomato industry of Mexico today is based on cultivars bred in the U.S. from stocks imported from Europe.

12. Peanuts. The U.S. market types are Spanish, Valencia, and Virginia Runner. The first was introduced from Spain in 1871 and the second probably came at the same time from the same source. The Valencia type is the one that reached Mexico from South America in pre-Columbian times and was the first to be widely distributed after European contact, reaching China and Madagascar in the 16th century. It is grown on only a small scale in the U.S. The runner type, thought to have come from Brazil, is by far the most important in this country. A. Chevalier even specified Bahia (Higgins 1951), but there are no records of the introduction (Gregory et al. 1951). At the present time 60% of the crop is produced by one cultivar, 88% by three cultivars, and over 90% by four cultivars. Of the four, two are runners and two Spanish (Hammons, 1976).

13. Barley. Spanish types were introduced early into New Mexico, Arizona, and California from Mexico. The coast variety selected from this material was the standard in California for many years, and Atlas was an important derivative. The barley-growing area of western New York was developed early from material out of Scotland. The Manchuria-Oderbrucker types that dominated the upper Mississippi Valley region for several decades came from Germany. Russian immigrants brought Stavropol to Kansas where it and its derivatives became important. "In some way not now clear, a winter barley, probably from Switzerland or the Balkans, was introduced into the mountain region of the southeastern states where it has long been grown as Tennessee Winter and Union Winter" (Harlan and Martini 1936). These several strains laid the foundation of the barley industry. Other important introductions include Club Mariout from Egypt (1904), and Trebi, selected out of a lot from Trebizond, Turkey, obtained in 1905. The smooth awned character in a number of cultivars can be traced to Lion, a selection out of material received from Taganrog, Russia in 1911.

14. Oats. Red Rustproof was for many years the most important variety grown in the U.S. and especially in the South. It came from Mexico about 1848, although seeds of

the Rustproof kind have been found in adobe bricks of California missions dating to 1797. "Nearly 50 American winter and spring oat varieties trace to Red Rustproof by either selection or hybridization" (Coffman, Murphy, and Chapman 1961). It has probably been a parent of over 100 cultivars worldwide. Some important selections out of it include Burt (1878), Fulghum (1892), and Kanota (1919) which together once occupied several million acres each year. Kherson was introduced from Russia by F.W. Taylor, of Nebraska in 1896, and such varieties as Iogold, Richland, Albion, State Pride, and Iowar were selected from it. Victoria came from Uruguay, with good resistance to crown rust, but high susceptibility to victoria blight. Bond came from Australia, resistant to crown rust (except race 45) and also to Victoria blight. Sources of resistance to race 45 of crown rust are Landhafer from Uruguay via Germany, Santa Fe from Argentina, and Trispernia from Romania via Canada. It seems the bulk of U.S. oat germ plasm came from Latin America and has only a remote relationship to any center of origin.

15. Sugarbeets. Early in the development of the sugarbeet industry, we were unable to produce our own seed, and imported it from Europe by the ton. From 1920 to 1933, for example, importation averaged 15 million pounds per year. U.S. cultivars now trace primarily to these stocks (Coons 1936).

In summary, one is struck by the narrow genetic bases of adapted sources of American germ plasm. Out of hundreds of thousands of introductions only a few yielded commercially successful derivatives. Some of the sources trace to gene centers, but most do not (see table 2). This is instructive in itself. Good germ plasm is where you find it. If you are looking for adapted materials, you will have the most success by looking in areas resembling yours climatically, or which are a bit more severe, and where the crop has been grown for a considerable time. If you are looking for disease resistance, you look in areas where the disease has been endemic for a long time. If you are looking for genetic stocks that would combine well with yours, there may be no way of predicting where to look, and it may be necessary to test everything. If you are looking for variability in general, gene centers are the most rewarding. It would be unwise to concentrate on gene centers to the exclusion of other sources. The task ahead is to sample, as best we can, the total range of variability in our major crops, and reserve the material for future generations.

Table 2. Primary Sources of U.S. Germ Plasm

	Crop	Probable Ultimate Origin	Main Sources of U.S. Germ Plasm
1.	Corn	Mexico-Guatemala	Indigenous flints and dents, in situ development
2.	Soybean	Northeast China	North and East China, Korea, Japan,
3.	Alfalfa	Southwest Asia	Chile, Germany, Russia, India, France, Peru, Egypt
4.	Wheat	Southwest Asia	North Europe, India, Russia, Italy, Australia
5.	Cotton	Mesoamerica (upland) So. America (long staple)	Mexico Bahama Island, Egypt
6.	Tobacco	So. America	So. America, West Indies
7.	Sorghum	Africa (Sudan-Chad)	Egypt, Sudan, Natal, So. Africa
8.	Potatoes	Andean Region, So. Am.	Europe
9.	Oranges	So. China-Indo-China	Azores, Brazil, in situ
10.	Rice	Southeast Asia	Honduras, Japan, Philippines, Madagascar
11.	Tomatoes	Peru or Mexico	England, France, in situ
12.	Peanuts	So. America	Spain, Brazil
13.	Barley	Southwest Asia	Mexico, Scotland, Germany, Russia, Balkans, Turkey
14.	Oats	Europe	Mexico, Uruguay, Russia Australia
15.	Sugarbeet	Europe	Europe

Geographic sources: The Americas (6); Southwest Asia (3);
   The Orient (3); Europe (2); Africa (1).
Botanical sources: Gramineae (6); Leguminosae (3); Solanaceae (3);
   Malvaceae (1); Rutaceae (1); Chenopodiaceae (1).
Ploidy levels: Diploids (7); Tetraploids (7), including durum wheat;
   Hexaploids (2).

After World War II

The Research and Marketing Act of 1946 was a promising start toward a more systematic assembly of genetic resources. Regional Plant Introduction Stations were established in the four regions and some money was made available for plant exploration. The National Seed Storage Laboratory was eventually established at Fort Collins in 1958 for the purpose of long term seed storage of important stocks (Burgess 1971). While these moves were encouraging and the flow of germ plasm into the country was increased, no systematic national plan for genetic resource management ever materialized. Exploration was, and still is, on an action and reaction basis. If a particular commodity should suffer severe loss or threat of loss to some disease or pest, enough pressure may be generated to squeeze a modest appropriation from the Congress to send out collectors to search for the needed resistance. Implementation of a systematic master plan for germ plasm assembly seems out of the question. Someone must be hurt before any action is taken (Harlan 1975).

The use of exotic germ plasm has been broadened considerably in recent decades. Disease, insect, and nematode resistance continue to be a major use of foreign germ plasm, but some of the other uses are illustrated below:

1. **Improvement in quality.** Genes regulating higher lysine content of maize protein were found among our genetic stock collections (Mertz et al. 1964). This led to a search for similar genes in other crops and for other quality controls. High lysine plus high protein was found in Ethiopian barley (Munck et al. 1970) and also in Ethiopian sorghum (Singh and Axtell 1973). High oil and better protein was transferred from wild to cultivated oats (Frey 1975, Frey et al. 1975). Higher soluble-solids (mostly sugars) were transferred from a wild green-fruited tomato to commercial canning types (Rick 1974). Higher polyunsaturation is being bred into oil crops (Harlan 1976). Lower oil and higher protein are being developed in soybean (Brim 1973). Low gossypol cottons are being tested, and stronger lint has been transferred from lintless wild cottons (Kerr 1951, Louant 1973).

2. **New cytoplasm and cytoplasmic sterile systems.** Commercial production of several crops has depended on the production of hybrids through cytoplasmic male sterile systems. The establishment of such systems has often depended on use of exotic cytoplasms. Since the 1970

epidemic of southern corn leaf blight, sources of alternative cytoplasms have been sought not only for corn, but for all crops using such procedures for hybrid production. In our sample of crops, these include corn, sorghum, and sugarbeets on a commercial scale, and wheat, cotton, alfalfa, and barley, at least in developmental stages.

3.   Modification of plant architecture. Sorghum was adapted to combine harvest before World War II by use of mutations for height that appeared spontaneously in sorghum fields. More recently, exotic germ plasm has been used to develop short-statured, lodging resistant, and fertilizer responsive wheat, barley, and rice. A major contribution to the processed tomato industry was the development of plants suitable for machine harvest. The ability of these plants to mature fruit synchronously is truly remarkable, and this feature is combined with resistance to several diseases and nematodes, plus acceptable quality. Corn and rice with upright leaves and single-stalked (uniculum) forms of barley, rice, and wheat are being explored for high plant populations. The development of monogerm sugarbeets was a great contribution toward mechanization of the crop and reduction of costs in thinning.

4.   Resistance to stress. Seedling cold tolerance for early planting has been stressed in corn and tomatoes; more cold tolerant sugarcanes through use of wild relatives are being developed. Sources of resistance to saline conditions, drouth, and wet soils have been identified in wild tomatoes (Rick 1973). By using wild tomatoes from the Galapagos Islands, lines have been developed so salt tolerant that they can be watered with sea water. Exotic germ plasm has been used in breeding each of the major crops for wider adaptation and resistance to various kinds of stress.

5.   Modified breeding systems. Modern potato breeding frequently involves reducing commercial tetraploids to diploids, making genetic manipulations at the diploid level, then raising the ploidy level again to tetraploid. Exotic diploid species are often used for the purpose. Genetic stocks are being used to develop cytogenetic male sterile systems in corn, that do not depend on any cytoplasm other than normal. Substitution lines, addition lines, reciprocal translocation stocks, trisomics, monosomics, nullisomics, and many other chromosome arrangements have been used to set up special breeding systems in wheat, corn, barley, tomatoes, cotton, and other crops. The art of chromosome engineering has improved substantially in recent years. New

techniques, including haploid production and tissue culture, offer great possibilities for the future.

6. Genetic conversion. One barrier to the use of tropical germ plasm has been photoperiod reaction. Many accessions of sorghum, for example, do not flower or flower too late to be used in breeding programs. A selected sample of such exotics has been and is being converted to usable types by crossing to adapted lines in the tropics. Since short-day reaction is dominant, the F_1 must be grown in tropics as well (in this case Puerto Rico). The F_2 is grown in Texas, early selections are made and returned to Puerto Rico for the first backcross. BC_1 is also short-day and is selfed in Puerto Rico before sending to Texas for the second round. This is repeated at least four times before material is suitable for use in the U.S. (Stephens et al. 1967). Tropical corns have been adapted by repeated selection for earlier types. This has made it possible to explore the genetic potential of ETO (Estación Tulio Ospino) lines from Colombia for improving and/or broadening corn belt germ plasms (Hallauer and Sears 1972), as well as tropical races of the Caribbean (Troyer and Brown 1972).

7. Use of wide crosses. It is often impossible to find the desired characters within the crop species, and it is necessary to attempt interspecific or even intergeneric crosses. These are being used more and more at an accelerated rate (Harlan 1976). Wild relatives of our crops have been used for all of the purposes mentioned above and more. Triticale is an attempt to synthesize an entirely new crop out of wheat and rye germ plasm. Triticales trace back before World War II, but are only now showing sufficient promise to attract world-wide attention. In this case the entire genome of rye is added to those of tetraploid or hexaploid wheat (Larter et al. 1968). A more common use of alien species is a controlled introgression which may result in greater yield, wider adaptation, or improved quality. Positive results have been obtained in tobacco, potatoes, oats, sugarcane, strawberries, grapes, and other crops. Extremely valuable genes for resistance to disease and pests have been extracted from wild relatives and inserted into wheat, cotton, tobacco, sorghum, potatoes, rice and tomatoes, to mention only a few of our most important crops (Harlan 1976).

In summary, we are using exotic germ plasm much more widely and more intensively than we used to. Any source of germ plasm within genetic reach may be useful and should be explored for useful genetic traits. The primary barrier to exploitation of germ plasm today is the inadequacy of our collections. Some are better than others, but all of them have gaps in geographic, ecological, and taxonomic coverage. All are especially weak and inadequate in the sampling of wild relatives.

Attention has been called repeatedly to the dangers of the situation; to the rapid erosion of genetic resources around the world and our persistent inaction as resources slip away year after year (Harlan 1972). Failure to assemble adequate genetic resources will place our agriculture in a far more vulnerable position than have the narrow genetic bases of our crops which have long been characteristic of American agriculture (Anon. 1972).

References

Anderson, E. and W.L. Brown. 1952. The history of the common maize varieties of the United States corn belt. Agric. Hist. 26: 2-8.

Anonymous. 1972. Genetic vulnerability of major crops. Nat. Acad Sciences ISBN 0-309-02030-1.

Ball, C.R. 1910. The history and distribution of sorghum. USDA Bull. No. 175. Washington. 63 pp.

Bolton, J.L., B.P. Goplen, and H. Baenziger. 1972. World distribution and historical developments. In: C.H. Hanson, ed. Alfalfa Science and Technology. Amer. Soc. Agron., Madison, Wis. pp. 1-34.

Boswell, V.R. 1937. Improvement and genetics of tomatoes, peppers, and eggplant. In: USDA Yearbook of Agriculture, Washington, pp. 176-206.

Brin, C.A. 1973. Quantitative genetics and breeding. In: B.E. Caldwell, R.W. Howell, R.W. Judd, and H.W. Johnson, eds. Soybeans: improvement, production, and uses. Amer. Soc. Agron., Madison, Wis., pp. 155-186.

Burgess, S. ed. 1971. The national program for conservation of crop germ plasm. Univ. Georgia Press, Athens 73 pp.

Carleton, M.A. 1920. The small grains. Macmillan, N.Y. 699 pp.

Clark, J.A. 1936. Improvement in wheat. In: USDA Yearbook of Agriculture, Washington. pp. 207-302.

Coffman, F.A., H.C. Murphy, and W.H. Chapman. 1961. Oat breeding In: F.A. Coffman, ed. Oats and Oat Improvement. Amer. Soc. Agron., Madison, Wis. pp. 263-329.

Coons, G.G. 1936. Improvement of the Sugarbeet. In: USDA Yearbook of Agriculture, Washington. pp. 625-656.

Frey, K.J. 1975. Heritability of groat-protein percentage in hexaploid oats. Crop Science 15: 227-279.

Frey, K.J., E.G. Hammond, and P.K. Lawrence. 1975. Inheritance of oil percentage in interspecific crosses of hexaploid oats. Crop Science 15: 94-95.

Garner, W.W., H.A. Allard, and E.E. Clayton. 1936. Superior germ plasm in tobacco. In: USDA Yearbook of Agriculture. pp. 785-830.

Gregory, W.C., B.W. Smith, and J.A. Yarbrough. 1951. Morphology. Genetics and breeding. In: The Peanut, the Unpredictable Legume. Natl. Fertilizer Assoc., Washington. pp. 28-88.

Hallauer, A.R. and J.H. Sears. 1972. Integrating exotic germplasm in corn belt maize breeding programs. Crop Science 12: 203-206.

Hammons, R.O. 1976. Peanuts: genetic vulnerability and breeding strategy. Crop Science 16(4): 527-530.

Hanson, C.H. and R.L. Davis. 1972. Highlights in the United States In: C.H. Hanson, ed. Alfalfa Science and Technology. Amer. Soc. Agron., Madison, Wis. pp. 35-51.

Harlan, H.V. and M.L. Martini. 1936. Problems and results in barley breeding. In: USDA yearbook of Agriculture. Washington. pp. 303-346.

Harlan, J.R. 1972. Genetics of disaster. J. Environ. Quality. 1: 212-215.

Harlan, J.R. 1975. Our vanishing genetic resources. Science 188: 618-622.

Harlan, J.R. 1976. Genetic resources in wild relatives of crops. Crop Science 16: 329-333.

Hartwig, E.E. 1973. Varietal development. In: Caldwell, R.W. Howell, R.W. Judd, and N.W. Johnson, eds. Soybeans: improvement, production and uses. Amer. Soc. Agron., Madison, Wis. pp. 187-210.

Higgins, B.B. 1951. Origin and early history of the peanut. In: The Peanut the Unpredictable Legume. Natl. Fertilizer Assoc., Washington. pp. 18-27.

Jenkins, J.A. 1948. The origin of the cultivated tomato. Econ. Bot. 2: 379-392.

Jones, J.W. 1936. Improvement in rice. In: USDA yearbook of Agriculture. Washington. pp. 415-454.

Karr, T. 1951. Transference of lint length and strength into upland cotton. Proc. 3rd Cotton Impr. Conf., Memphis (Tenn.).

Larter, E., T. Tsuchiya, and L. Evans. 1968. Breeding and genetics of triticale. In: K.W. Finlay and K.W. Shepherd, eds. Proc. 3rd Internat. Wheat Genet. Symp., Canberra. pp. 93-101.

Louant, B.P. 1973. Recherches sur les possibilitées d'améliorer le contonnier par l'introgréssion directe de caractères provenant de Gossypium raimondii Ulbr. Publ. Inst. Natl. Etude Agron. Congo 116.

Martin, J.H. 1936. Sorghum improvement. In: USDA Yearbook of Agriculture, Washington. pp. 523-560.

Mertz, E.T., O.E. Nelson, and L.S. Bates. 1964. Mutant gene that changes protein composition and increases lysine content of maize endosperm. Science 145: 279-280.

Munck, L., K.E. Karlsson, A. Hagberg, and B.O. Eggum. 1970. Gene for improved nutritional value in barley seed protein. Science 168: 985-987.

Quisenberry, K.S. and L.P Reitz. 1974. Turkey wheat: the cornerstone of an empire. Agric. Hist. 48: 98-114.

Rick, C.M. 1973. Potential genetic resources in tomato species: clues from observations in native habitats.

In: A.M. Srb eds. Genes, Enzymes, and Populations. Plenum, N.Y. pp. 255-269.

Rick, C.M. 1974. High soluble-solids content in large-fruited tomato lines derived from a wild green-fruited species. Hilgardia 42: 493-510.

Singh, R. and J.D. Axtell. 1973. High lysine mutant gene (hl) that improves protein quality and biological value of grain sorghum. Crop Science 13: 535-539.

Stephens, J.C., F.R. Miller, and D.T. Rosenow. 1967. Conversion of alien sorghums to early combine genotypes. Crop Sci. 7: 396.

Stevenson, F.J. and C.F. Clark. 1937. Breeding and genetics in potato improvement. In: USDA Yearbook of Agriculture, Washington. pp. 405-444.

Traub, H. and T.R. Robinson. 1937. Improvement of subtropical fruit crops: citrus. In: USDA Yearbook of Agriculture, Washington. pp. 749-826.

Troyer, A.F. and W.L. Brown. 1972. Selection for early flowering in corn. Crop Science 12: 302-304.

USDA. 1973. Agricultural Statistics, 1978. U.S. Govt. Print. Off. Washington.

Wallace, H.A. and W.L. Brown. 1956. Corn and its early fathers. Michigan State Univ. Press, East Lansing.

Ware, J.O. 1936. Plant breeding and the cotton industry In: USDA Yearbook of Agriculture, Washington. pp. 657-744.

11. Germplasm Conservation Toward the Year 2000: Potential for New Crops and Enhancement of Present Crops

Extinction of a species or a genetic line represents an irreversible loss and results in permanent impoverishment of global resources. Throughout the world, people increasingly consume food, take medicine, and employ industrial materials that owe their production to genetic resources of biological organisms. The imperative for genetic conservation develops from three processes in our current world:

1. An increasing human population which leads to further alteration of natural ecosystems and the expansion of food producing agriculture.

2. The widespread adoption of elite crop plant germplasm and agricultural technology which promotes genetic uniformity, sometimes worldwide.

3. The centers of genetic variability of agricultural crop species are moving from natural systems and primitive agriculture to gene banks and breeders' working collections with the liabilities that a concentration of resource implies.

Given the needs of the future, genetic resources can be reckoned among society's most valuable raw material. Any reduction in the diversity of resources narrows society's scope to respond to new problems and opportunities. To the extent that we cannot be certain what needs may arise in the future, it makes sense to keep our options open. This conservation rationale applies to the earth's endowment of useful plants more than to almost any other category of natural resource. It is difficult to visualize a challenge more profound in its implications yet less appreciated by the general public than plant genetic resources.

The world's human population could not survive at its present density were it not for cultivated plants and

domesticated animals.   Since approximately 80% of our
calories are supplied by plants, the primacy of plants in
meeting the food need is evident.   The number of plants that
actually feeds the world's population is small.   Approximately half of all human energy is derived from the cereals
rice, wheat, and maize alone.   Plants are also used for
fiber and shelter needs.   A good part of the world is
clothed in cotton and the number of woods used in shelter
and building construction is not that numerous.

Food security will be a more obvious challenge between
now and the end of the century.   By the year 2000 the human
population of more than 6 billion will require an agricultural production 60% greater than that harvested in 1980.
Most of this population increase will take place in the
developing countries where demand for food and agricultural
products will double.   The problems of an increasingly
precarious food supply and rural poverty is expected to
increase the pressure on scarce land for arable farming and
meager resources for agricultural inputs (IUCN 1980).
According to conservative FAO estimates there would be an
increase in the number of seriously undernourished to some
600 to 650 million (FAO 1981).

Since new arable land in the developing nations will
become steadily more scarce, higher yields from land already
in production will be the only way to support the population
increase (CEQ 1981).   Higher yields mean using more energy
for fertilizer, plowing, and lifting water and improved
plant material (Abelson 1975).   Breeding of better crop
plants will be the focal point around which all strategies
to increase crop yields will develop.   It is the positive
response of these improved seeds and other plant material to
soil, water, fertilizer, pest, weather, and social institutions that will determine the success of the future
agriculture.

Historically humans have used worldwide only about 5000
plant species to meet food and fiber needs.   This small
number is less than a fraction of one percent of the total
world flora.   As the human population has grown in number we
have depended increasingly on a shorter list containing the
most productive plants.   Today only about 150 plant species
are important in meeting the calorie needs of humans worldwide.   The short list of the most used foods are what stand
between us and the estimated worldwide carrying capacity in
pre-agricultural times of about 25 million humans.   This
list contains:

CEREALS	LEGUMES	OIL SEEDS	ROOT CROPS
wheat	soybeans	coconut	potatoes
rice	peanut	cottonseed	sweet potato
maize	common beans	sunflower	cassava
barley	pea		yam and taro
oats	chickpeas		
sorghum	cowpeas		
millets			
rye			

SUGAR CROPS	VEGETABLES	FRUITS
sugar cane	tomatoes	banana
sugar beet	cabbage	oranges
grapes (wine)	onions	apples and
mango	squash	pears
		mellons

The cereals represent twice the tonage of all the other crops (if the potato with their high water content is discounted) and nearly three times the calories. Both tea and coffee are major world crops but these caffeine beverages are not included because they add essentially no calories to human nutrition. This list is primarily a calorie list and does not recognize the important role of low calorie vegetables and fruits in supplying vitamins, minerals, and protein to human nutrition. The list also does not include regional foods that locally may supply more than 1/2 of the calories consumed and, in addition, both pasture forages and fiber crops are omitted. Figure 1 summarizes food crops by calorie contribution and Table 1 lists crops by weight, protein content and calorie contribution.

I seriously doubt that there remains an as yet undiscovered major food plant, so before any survey of potential new crops I wish to outline three processes that affect the crops we now cultivate. These three processes—genetic erosion, genetic vulnerability, and genetic wipeout—are not mutually exclusive but are, in fact, interlocked by the demands of an increasing human population and rising expectations.

●   GENETIC EROSION - The technological bind of improved varieties is that they eliminate the resource upon which they are based. Over the past 10,000 years crop plants have proliferated an innumerable number of locally adapted genotypes. These land races and folk

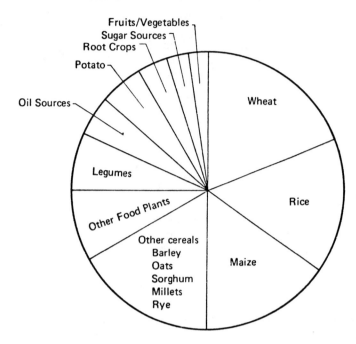

FIGURE 1.   Human calorie sources from plants.

Table 1.   Major global crop harvest (first 25 crops by weight)

	Production (millions of metric tons)	Approx. Water (%)	Protein (%)	World Calories (%)	World Protein (%)
Wheat	360	10	12.1	21.1	27.9
Rice	320	10	6.1	20.3	12.5
Maize	300	10	8.2	18.8	15.7
Potato	300	75	1.4	3.3	2.7
Barley	170	10	8.7	10.4	9.5
Sweet potato	130	70	1.2	2.1	1.0
Cassava	100	70	0.5	1.5	0.3
Sorghum	50	10	7.0	2.9	2.5
Millet	45	10	8.9	2.6	2.6
Grape	60	75	0.5	0.6	0.2
Soybean	60	10	30.8	4.3	11.8
Oats	50	10	12.9	3.4	4.1
Sugar cane	50	70	0	0.6	0
Banana	35	70	0.7	0.4	0.2
Tomato	35	90	1.0	0.1	0.2
Sugar beet	30	70	0	0.4	0
Rye	30	10	10.9	1.8	2.1
Orange	30	80	0.7	0.2	0.1
Coconut	30	50	3.2	1.8	0.6
Apple	20	80	0.1	0.2	0
Yams	20	70	1.6	0.3	0.2
Peanut	20	10	23.0	2.0	2.9
Watermelon	20	95	0.2	0	0
Cabbage	15	90	1.0	0.1	0.1
Onion	15	90	1.2	0.1	0.1

Baseline is FAO (1976).
It is assumed that these are all consumed directly be people.

varieties of indigenous and peasant agriculture have
been the genetic reservoir for the plantbreeder in crop
improvement. Suddenly this genetic diversity is being
replaced with a relatively small number of varieties
bred for high yields and other adaptations necessary
for high input agriculture. In addition, the scarcity
of land is forcing changes in land use and agricultural
practices resulting in the disappearance of habitat to
maintain wild progenitors and weedy forms of our basic
food plants. As a result of these two trends, there is
urgent need to collect and conserve the diverse genetic
materials that remain. In a world where per capita
resources are decreasing as the human population grows,
the concept of a sustainable future is becoming
increasingly more important. Biological diversity is
one of the components of any sustainable future that
includes humans.

● GENETIC VULNERABILITY – Genetic vulnerability is the
risk of high input agriculture with commercial food
crop varieties typical of developed nations. Genetic
erosion, the gradual persistent loss of plant genetic
resources, is most typically, but not exclusively, a
phenomenon of land races in developing nations.
Genetic vulnerability is the "thin ice" of a narrow
genetic base. Never before have there been such widespread monocultures (dense, uniform stands of billions
of plants) covering thousands of acres, all genetically
similar. The narrowness of the genetic base is responsible for greater risk of crop failure, as occurred in
the wheat stem rust of 1954 or the southern corn blight
of 1970 in the U.S. The Irish potato famine in the
1840s is a classic example of genetic vulnerability.

● GENETIC WIPEOUT – The third threat to crop plant
germplasm is the rapid and wholesale destruction of
genetic resources. Social disruptions such as political instability or crop failure and famine can eliminate genetic resources. Quite literally, the genetic
heritage of a millenium in a particular valley can
disappear in a single bowl of porridge if the seeds are
cooked and eaten instead of saved as seed stock.
Equally dramatic is the discarding of a genetic
collection because a curator retires or the collection
is no longer of use to the institution. A classic case
of the above is the USDA melon breeding program. The
crop was threatened by mildew problems and plant
explorers assembled a world collection of mellons. The
genes for resistance were located and bred into

the crop and the seed of susceptible melon types discarded. No sooner had the collection been thrown away
than attacks of virus threatened the crop and plant
explorers went out for a second collection. At the
present time there is no institutional arrangements
by which the perpetuation of genetic collections
can be coordinated. The U.S. has no policy, no
clearing house for privately and/or publicly held
research and working collections of genetic stocks
(Wilkes 1983).

Crop Plants are Domesticated Plants

Most domesticated plants and all the food plants are
the product of a long selection process by which humans have
produced a plant that is totally dependent upon our care
for survival. We call this evolutionary process domestication. In the process of domestication, food plants have
quite literally crossed a threshold. Their survival is
keyed to human preparation of the ground, to decreased
competition with other plants, to sowing of the seed in the
proper season, to protection of the plants during their
growth and finally to the collecting of their seed. The
process of domestication has made these plants our depen-
dents, but the human population has increased to such
numbers that we could not possibly meet our food needs with
wild plants. Ironically, we in turn are held captive by our
domesticated food plants; that is we are totally dependent
on the high yields of these cultivated plants (Figure 2).

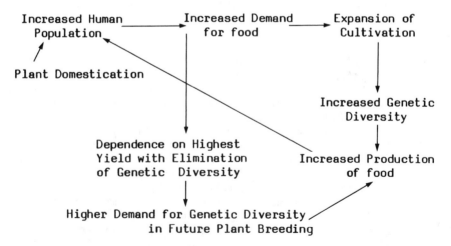

Figure 2. Plant domestication, genetic diversity and human
population growth.

Plant Genetic Resources

The process of plant breeding is a dynamic one of genetic selection in response to changing diseases, parasites, agricultural techniques and human use. As the human population increased, the growing of these crops expanded into many different environments and an enormous wealth of genetic variation was preserved over the centuries in locally adapted races. Only a small sample of this variation is now employed in the elite breeding stocks of leading crop varieties and much of the rest is still located in native indigenous traditional agriculture which is rapidly disappearing (Harlan 1971, 1975, Frankel and Bennett 1970, Frankel and Hawkes 1975, Whyte and Julen 1963).

Over large areas of the globe the genetic uniformity of a few varieties is displacing the thousands of local varieties. The process is a paradox in social and economic development; the product of technology (plant breeding for yield and uniformity) displaces the resource upon which the technology is based (genetic diversity of new and potentially useful genes found in locally adapted land races). Our current condition might be compared to a house where rocks from the foundation are used to repair a leak in the roof. This in itself is not bad, it does solve the immediate problem but if repeated over a period of time an irreversible liability is created (Wilkes & Wilkes 1972).

The genetic diversity of indigenous traditional agriculture has been the reservoir from which many of the strains and valuable genes used by plant breeders in the last 50 years have come. Almost every part of the globe has been tapped for useful genes which intensified or changed some plant characteristics, conveyed increased resistance to fungal diseases or insect attack, or improved the durability or nutritional qualities of the harvest.

Only a small fraction of this rapidly disappearing variation has been sampled and included in the present leading crop varieties.

For convenience, germplasm resources can be classified into seven distinct categories:

- varieties of cultivars in current use;
- obsolete varieties of cultivars;
- primitive cultivars or land races of native agriculture;
- wild and weedy taxa, near relatives of cultivated crops;

- special genetic stocks, which are the tools of plant breeders;
- induced mutations by x-rays or some other high energy or chemical mutagenic means; and
- coadapted genetic stocks where two forms of a crop, two distinct crops or a crop and symbiont, such as a nodule forming bacteria, are grown together.

The varieties or cultivars in current use have generally undergone a rather rigorous selection process by plant breeders and are more or less homgeneous. These varieties possess a "highly tuned" set of genes but a considerably narrowed gene base over the native land races from which they have come. These advanced varieties are the ones most widely and frequently used as parents in current breeding programs or in introducing a variety into an area of comparable climate (NAS 1972). The fact that most exotic introductions do poorly have convinced many breeders to think of them as worthless. The truth is that seldom are introductions valuable as a superior variety when well-established elite lines already exist for the region. However, introduced exotics should be considered valuable as parents and this requires careful screening and evaluation, an effort that has low priority as labor costs increase. Yet the introduction of superior genes is probably one of the most cost effective R&D payoffs in today's markets. At the present time we have almost no facilities and/or institutional arrangements to effectively evaluate the genetic potential held by gene banks. Currently there is a national and worldwide need for a new kind of genetist — an evaluation and characterization specialist — who would take the first step in any breeding for enhancement program.

Obsolete varieties are advanced cultivars from the past that have been displaced by newer releases. Often this older material was one of the parents for the new release. Both special genetic stocks and induced mutational stocks are comparable to obsolete varieties in the amounts of genetic variation they possess.

Primitive varieties or land races are the real treasure house because they are the largest repository of genes for a crop, but also the largest unknown because 1) they are usually heterogeneous, and 2) little data exist on their morphological, biochemical and genetic traits, or their responses to pest or environmental stress. Most coadapted genetic stocks are "special case" land races where two distinct genetic potentials have been coadapted to each other. There are not many of these systems left in the world but genetically they are very valuable.

Generally land races perform poorly under inputs of high fertilizer, water, and intensive cultivation and are replaced by the "new seed." On the other hand, there is a fairly wide variation in the ability of land races to survive in fluctuating environments, to withstand cold, drought, disease, insect damage and other such variables. After all, most land races represent accumulated mutational events integrated and balanced in the real world over thousands of years. It is with the genes that they possess that the story of modern plant breeding has been created (Hodge 1956, Klose 1950).

Conservation in Perpetuity

Conservation in perpetuity of plant genetic resources can take three forms:

- Entire biomes (the entire preservation of vast tracts with in situ conservation of animals and plants). This level of preservation will be extremely important in slowing the rate of species extinction but will have little impact on genetic resources of useful plants (IUCN 1980).

- In situ preservation as land races and wild relatives where genetic diversity exists and where wild/weedy forms are present and often hybridizing with the cultivated varieties. These are evolutionary systems that are difficult for plant breeders to simulate and should not be knowingly destroyed. Their preservation probably is not possible but deceleration of their disappearance will give us more time to better understand how these systems evolved. Considerable potential for creative institutional arrangements exist for in situ preservation, especially in the developing countries (Wilkes and Wilkes 1972, Prescott Allen and Proscott Allen 1981).

- Ex situ preservation as seed or in vitro cell lines stored in gene banks under appropriate conditions for long term storage. This is the mode for the preservation of most genetic resources of agricultural crops. Such a system draws genes out of circulation and therefore to be useful requires documentation and evaluation so that a plant breeder will have enough information to know what to request. Information management will be as important as the physical arrangements of the gene bank. Gene banks slow down crop plant evolution and so the hybridization and breeding process becomes a necessary part in making ex situ preservation useful. Ex situ preservation has three aspects: (1) exploitation, collection and banking; (2) evaluation and documentation; and (3) breeding and enhancement (Jensen 1962, Thompson and Brown 1972, USDA 1981, Wilkes 1983). Currently we are most weak in the areas of evaluation, documentation and enhancement (U.S. Government Ag. Res. Policy Comm. 1973, U.S. Government 1973, Vavilov 1926, Wilkes 1977, Forum 1983).

Undervalued Plant Genetic Resources

Biological diversity is the raw material of the plant breeding process and traditionally this resource has been free; collected as seed in primitive land races in peasant fields around the world, sent in envelopes on request, stored in a gene bank on the possibility that some person will have need of the plants in the future. The plant explorer who underwent the hardships and dangers never cashed in on the useful genes collected, the plant introduction officer never became a hero for keeping the thousands of envelopes catalogued separately and systematically, and the gene bank personnel were never thanked for maintaining safe storage conditions every hour of every day, year after year. Biological resources are renewable and historically humans could own a tree or horse but once they had given seed of the tree away or sold the colt of the horse, they did not traditionally have claim to the seed or the progeny of the colt. Traditionally, plant genetic resources have been a heritage not subject to the narrow concept of ownership. Because it has been a renewable resource subject to the rapid geometric increase of biological reproduction there has not been a measured stewardship to preserve the heritage. Suddenly the world is changing and these old assumptions are not holding true. With the advent of plant breeders rights, genetic resources can be owned and, in the absence of management intervention, the genetic heritage of crops can be significantly narrowed.

To better understand why crop plant genetic resources have been undervalued I think we need to look at the context in which they are used. Certainly plant breeding is of primary importance. Plant breeding is a method of germplasm enhancement of already existing allelic variation, of creative recombination through hybridization of differing genotypes and intense artificial selection and recombination of plant forms that probably would not survive or occur in the wild.

The plant breeder is at the research and development end of the use of plant genetic resources and that such a small cadre can maintain a constantly improving list of crop varieties is a tribute to the value of germplasm. For lack of a better scale, the effectiveness of this research and development can be measured by the ratio of researcher over consumer served. There are approximately 500 scientific man years in USDA and USDA/State cooperative breeding programs in the U.S. The exact number of plant breeders for crop plants in the private sector is not known to me but probably is not larger than those in the public sector. Since U.S. agriculture feeds an excess of 500 million (our population plus exports), the effectiveness ratio for public sector plant breeding is 10^6:1, (one million to one) an efficiency ratio for research and development few institutions or industries could match.

Knowing what is in the world collection has been one of the main stumbling blocks to their use and the second has been the high cost of growing it out every couple of years. Lastly, there have not been many rewards for the people who collected, introduced, and maintained genes in crop collections. The payoffs come too late for personal satisfaction or public recognition. Hiproly barley (CI 3947 and CI 4362) was introduced from Ethiopia and made a part of the USDA world collection of small grains in 1924. It wasn't until 46 years later that the high lysine and total protein were discovered in these accessions. Opaque-2, a mutant maize of an Enfield, Conn., farmer's field (1922) was studied by Singleton and Jones (1938) as a new endosperm gene and maintained in their collection of mutants. It was not especially valued until the 1960s when it was discovered to possess a gene for high lysene (Reitz 1976), an essential protein for humans, classically low in maize diets. The impact of a gene depends on it being discovered and on it being valued. Values change and currently "worthless genes" might hold the key to overcoming a vulnerability in the year 2000.

The critical role of gene banking has been one of the least appreciated concepts in the agricultural research community and genetic diversity is still generally under-value because it isn't easy to locate useful genes in exotic materials. Once located, it is then a slow process to acclimate them in elite lines. In these gene banks a tremendous amount of unevaluated genetic variation, which is not of any currently known use, is being stored on the premise that it might be needed at same time in the future. But genes held in gene banks are worthless unless valued by plant breeders, and to accomplish this there must be

evaluation of all existing collections.   Two questions
arise: (1) Will it be maintained until it is needed and
once needed can it be mobilized (i.e., found in the collection fast enough because evaluation has been sufficiently
accurate and/or detailed to find it in the vast library of
genes)? and (2) Will it be freely available to all parties
from the evaluation team and/or gene bank?   Currently we
have no assurance that in the future these collections will
be freely and openly maintained.

Clearly realizing our dependence on genetic resources
creates a sense of humility which in the arrogance of our
accomplishments we have tried to ignore.   In the words of
Sir Otto Frankel: "To an unprecedented degree, this decision of vast consequence for the future of our planet is in
the hands of perhaps 2 or 3 generations...No longer can we
claim evolutionary innocence... We have acquired evolutionary responsibility" (Frankel 1974).

Another and very disturbing aspect is that plant germplasm might become a controlled commodity.   For thousands of
years the genetic heritage of our crops has been a commons
and passed freely from one generation to another, one
country to another.   The possibility exists to lose this
"commons" because we didn't think germplasm preservation
important and since it was a "free" genetic heritage from
the past, we assumed we would always have it indefinitely
into the future.   Without the free and open exchange of
genetic stock, the creative processes of plant breeding
could come to a halt.   The process of combining two plants
into one, as in the rye x wheat Triticale hybrids, or
transfer of drought stress resistance from other plants into
maize, or the development of nitrogen fixing roots on the
basic cereals, would become the property of persons or
corporations.   My personal view is that naturally occurring
genes are "commons," while specially constructed genotypes
are appropriate for patent protection.   There is controversy
surrounding this issue and the reader is referred to Mooney
(1980) and Lappe and Collins (1979) for reading from the
radical left and Cooper (1980), patent lawyer, Washington,
D.C., for an indepth review of the law and the patent system
as it applies to the "new biology."

New and Potential Crops

The second topic of this paper "New and Potential
Crops" is a recurring theme that distracts from the real
issue.   When we change our focus to look at the "new and
potential crops" our focus on the proven genetic diversity
fades.   Most of the suitable food crops have been discovered

and the major food crops today are essentially the same as the major crops of a century ago. In the last hundred years the biggest change has been the decrease in the acreage in oats due to the decline in importance of the horse and the use of the gasoline powered automobile. To look for new and wonderful food plants is a Pollyannaish dream which distracts us from the fact we should be preserving rare and nearly extinct forms of wheat from Ethiopia and Afghanistan or similarly rare races of maize from Mexico.

The major shift away from oats is a good example of the forces that will change the importance of a crop plant. Oats were grown not as a human food but as a horse feed. (Currently alfalfa is one of the most important crop plants worldwide but it isn't a primary human food, but a secondary one, because it is grown for livestock.) Starting about 1910, oats were displaced by a change in technology — the invention of the automobile. The automobile in turn created a demand for rubber wheels and plantation rubber became a major crop in the tropics. Probably the automobile will change our use of farmland in the future because of a demand for alternate fuels such as alcohol. The point to be made is that changing technology and the demands of the human population on the environment will create the interest and demand for new crops. Most of these crops will not be food related.

Most of our good cropland worldwide is already being utilized so many of these new industrial crops will have to compete with established food crops for land, water and fertilizers. New crops will not necessarily increase agricultural production. Examples of displacement are sugar cane for alcohol production (Brazil) or alcohol from grain (U.S.) used to fuel the automobile.

A second aspect of "New and Potential Crops" is to guess in what areas they are most likely to be discovered. The most obvious place to discover new crops is to look in new places. It is doubtful that any new major crop plant will be found in Europe or North America but it is quite likely that one or more might be found in the humid tropical forest of the world because this is the area with the greatest number of species and the least known flora. Of the total number of species living in the humid tropics probably only 1/6 have been identified and catalogued (AAAS 1981). The third aspect of "New and Potential Crops" is to discover new plant resources for improving the human diet worldwide or discovering a new industrial plant. Most probably these discoveries will be in the tropics.

Table 2. Priorities for further-germplasm collections for food plants of the humid tropics (first two groups) as listed by the International Board for Plant Genetic Resources

Priority Groups	Americas	Africa	Asia	Pacific
First	Maize Phaseolus beans Tree fruits and nuts Vegetables Cassava Sweet potato	Finger millet Starchy banana and plantains Rice (O. glaberrima) Coffee Tree fruits and nuts Vegetables Cassava Sweet potato	Finger millet Coconut Sugar cane Maize Starchy banana and plantains Rice Tree fruits and nuts Vegetables Sweet potato	Breadfruit Sugar cane Yam Taro Coconut Starchy banana and plantains
Second	Peanut South American oil palms Cocoa	Cowpea Bananas Bambara groundnut	Peanut Chickpea Vigna spp. Winged bean Banana Cassava Soybean	

IBPGR (1981).
Three additional priority groups (third, fourth, fifth) are listed by IBPGR.

Species Diversity in the Humid Tropics

Whereas genetic diversity is a measure of the variety of genes in a population, species diversity is a measure of the variety of species in a habitat. Species diversity in the humid tropics offers many utilitarian benefits, although much yet remains to be discovered (NAS 1982).

The tropical moist forest almost certainly contains many wild relatives of modern food plants (bananas, peanut, pineapple, cassava, cacao, coffee, rubber, yams, and many oil and fiber palms) that are still unknown. Once discovered, they may be used by plant breeders. During this century genetic materials from the wild have saved several important tropical crops including bananas, sugar cane, cacao, and coffee.

Species diversity also makes possible wholly new uses for plants. Examples here are the fish poisons—derived from <u>Derris</u> spp. (Asian moist tropics) and <u>Lonchocarpus</u> spp. (American moist tropics)—which are the basis of many insecticides.

Pharmaceuticals are often chemically complex, and the likelihood of finding plants with complex chemistry is much better in the moist tropics than elsewhere (Myers 1983).

Given future needs, genetic resources can be reckoned among society's more valuable raw materials. The fundamental issue, however, is that the greatest genetic diversity is in the humid tropics now. Any reduction in the diversity of resources narrows the scope of society's response to new problems and opportunities.

One of the simplest and most cost-effective ways to assist humid tropical countries in preservation of genetic resources is to support the ongoing efforts of major international institutions, especially the International Board for Plant Genetic Resources (IBPGR) and the International Union for the Conservation of Nature and Natural Resources (IUCN). Their priorities for collections are listed in Table 2.

The IBPGR is an autonomous, international, scientific organization operating under the aegis of the Consultative Group on International Agricultural Resarch (CGIAR). The IBPGR was established in 1974 and its executive secretariate is provided by the Food and Agriculture Organization of the United Nations. The basic function of the IBPGR is to promote an international network of genetic resources

centers to further the collection, conservation, documentation, evaluation, and use of plant germplasm.

IUCN is an independent, international organization with
a membership derived from sovereign states and international
and national agencies, whose purpose is to promote the
conservation of wildlife species and their habitats.
Through its World Conservation Strategy, formulated in 1980
(IUCN, 1980), it hopes to maintain essential natural processes and life-support systems, preserve the genetic diversity
essential for protecting and improving cultivated plants and
livestock and for scientific and medical purposes, and
sustain species and ecosystems that support productive rural
communities and major industries.

Improving the Plants of the Humid Tropics and New Crops

Half the world's population is engaged in agriculture,
mostly in the tropics and subtropics, yet the plant-breeding
arsenals for temperate-zone plants and tropical plants are
very different. The migration of European peoples around
the world spread temperate crop varieties to diverse habitats far from where they originated. The only migrations of
tropical peoples were as cheap laborers, not free farmers:
Africans to the Americas (sugarcane and cotton), Tamils to
Ceylon (tea) and Malaya (to tap rubber). No substantial
exchange of tropical crops (plantation crops excepted) has
taken place since the early introductions of the Portuguese
and Spanish. Despite the potential of tropical American
plants for the Old World (avocados for one), and Old World
plants for the New, there is no systematic exchange or
experimentation with acclimatization of tropical fruits and
vegetables.

Until very recently, the payoff from plant breeding of
tropical crops (except for rice and some plantation crops)
has been small. The agricultural stations needed to test
the acclimatization of crops and to carry out variety trials
are very sparse. Promising candidates for inten-
sive-breeding experiments include: tropical yams (Africa,
Asia, the Americas); pigeon peas, cowpeas, and other
legumes; tropical palms (oil palm excepted); crops designed
specifically for companion planting (legume and root crops)
and plants that improve tropical soils; Asian and New World
minor fruit trees; and N-fixing crops for wet rice
cultivation. Because 75% of the world's lesser crops are
grown and consumed in tropical countries, the industrial
nations have tended to ignore them both as sources of
nutrition and as germplasm resources for the future. The
large number of exceptional and underexploited fruits in

both Southeast Asia and the American tropics attest to lack of attention (Dodds 1963). Tropical fruits are a neglected resource. Many of the New World fruits have not diffused to the Old World, and the lesser fruits (other than citrus and bananas) of Southeast Asia are not found in the Americas.

The potential for research with tropical legumes is substantial. They are the most important daily protein source in many tropical countries. About 75% of the world's food legumes are grown and consumed in tropical countries (Ruthenberg 1976). The other major plant protein source in many of these diets is local leafy vegetables, mostly cultivated (Grubben 1977). Clearly, the demographic increases and technological progress of people in the tropics are restructuring natural ecosystems. Given present trends, the tropics will probably be the most altered regions of the globe in the twenty-first century. Without attention to conservation, the result may be irreversible erosion of genetic resources of the region, a decrease in the resilience of the existing systems, and diminution of the public-service function of vast tracts of tropical forest.

The Value of Plants from the Tropics

The problem of disappearing species could eventually be recognized as the great "sleeper issue" in the last decades of the 20th century (Eckholm 1978) (NAS 1978). It is difficult to visualize a challenge more profound in its implications, yet less appreciated by the general public, than that entailed in the wholesale elimination of species and their genetic resources now taking place in the tropics (NAS 1975).

To give an idea of the economic values involved, peanuts worldwide have suffered from a leaf-spot disease, a problem that has proved surmountable only through resistant varieties. This needed resistance was found in wild forms (such as Arachis monticola, A. batizocoi, and A. vilosa) from the tropical forest of Amazonia and has an annual value estimated by the International Crops Research Institute for Semi-Arid Tropics (ICRISAT) of $500 million (U.S.). In another instance, two species of wild green tomatoes, Lycopersicon chmielewskii and L. parviflorum discovered in an isolated area of the highlands of Peru in the early 1960s, have contributed genes for marked increase in fruit pigmentation and soluble-solids content worth nearly $5 million (U.S.) per year to the tomato-processing industry (Iltis 1981). Similar large-scale benefits of wild-relative germplasm could be documented for the tropical crops of rubber, coconuts, and oil palm (Frankel and Soule 1981) and for tropical forage species (CIAT 1980).

In addition to the many wild relatives of food plants, humid tropical forests constitute a wealth of drug-yielding plants. The plants of the tropics probably possess some of the most complex biochemistry in the plant kingdom. At least 70% of all plants known to possess anti-cancer properties (3,000 species in all) exist in the tropical humid forest. It is on these grounds that the U.S. National Cancer Institute believes that the widespread elimination of tropical forests represent an irreplaceable loss.

Another drug category of growing importance, those that serve as contraceptives and abortifacients, are also known from the tropical forest. An example is the rhizomes of a climbing vine, the Mexican yam, which yields virtually the world's entire supply of naturally derived diosgenin, from which a variety of sex hormone combinations are prepared, including "the pill." By the mid-1970s the world was using up to 180 tons of diosgenin per year; by the mid-1980s the amount could rise to as much as 500 tons, and if all women at risk in the 1990s used "the pill" the demand would be about 3000 tons. It now seems probable that chemical synthesis will replace the use of the yam as the starting material but the case still holds for the importance of this plant and others like it.

These are not the only drugs from the tropics. I could continue with arrow poisons used in cardiac medicine or fish poisons used in insecticides or the plant source for cocaine. All of the products have come from the tropics.

Yet another category of products derived from humid tropical forest are the specialist materials for industrial use. The range is wide and for some there are no quality substitutes from other sources. From tropical forests come latex, gums, camphor, dammars, resins, dyes, and ethereal oils. One group of industrial products that is receiving a fresh new look includes oils and lubricants. Many forest plants bear oil-rich seeds and/or fruits and the tropical palms are especially productive.

The palms as a group are the most significant multi-use plants of the tropics but their productivity is not well known or appreciated in the temperate region. In recent years, crop improvement of the African oil palm in Asia has led to spectacular productivity increases of this palm. Several tropical palms of comparable potential are known from the Americas that exist either as wild or little

cultivated palms.   These species are "uncut gems" in terms
of their potential.

Bukriti palm (<u>Maurtia flexuosa</u> L.) is perhaps the most
abundant palm in the Americas but it is not commercially
exploited.   Yet many products — starch-fruit-fiber and wood
—could be obtained from it on a large scale.   Pejibaye
(<u>Guillielma gasipaes</u> (HBK) LH Bailey) on the other hand is
not as much a utility palm as one worth growing because of
its chestnut-like fruit which is a choice package of carbo-
hydrates, oil, protein, vitamins and minerals.   Other palms,
Babassu (<u>Orbignya margiana</u>, Barb. Rodr) and Jessenia
(<u>Jessenia polycarpa</u> Karst.) to name two, bear edible oils of
high quality which are currently little exploited.

The palms are not the only oil source in the tropics.
Brief mention of one is the leaf wax from <u>Calathea lutea</u>
(Aublet) Schultes which is a superior protective wax of
complex chemistry difficult to manufacture on an industrial
scale.   An equally significant lipid plant, jojoba from the
American southwest, possesses a liquid wax which is impossible to produce synthetically on a commercial basis.   The
jojoba wax is the best replacement for sperm whale oil as a
lubricant with unique properties in the tool and machinery
industries.

This is but a short list and there are many of as yet
unexploited or under utilized crops in the tropics (NAS
1979).

The **fourth** way to look at "New and Potential Crops" is
to ask what are the real plant needs of humans that are not
being met with our present assemblage of plants.   Clearly
protein is one of the food materials in short supply and
improved quick-growing, protein-rich vegetable crops such as
the pseudo-cereals <u>Amaranthus</u> spp. and quinoa offer tremendous potential, especially in the tropics (see tables 3 and
4).   The root crops of the tropics are generally protein
short and maybe the tubers of the winged bean will improve
the diet of these tuber dependent diets.   Certainly the
transfer of nitrogen fixing nodules to the cereals will
revolutionize food production.   The creation of more drought
stress resistant plants would go far to improve the lot of
peoples that live in arid regions.   Fuel or round wood for
cooking is in many regions becoming as expensive as food.

All of these wants turned into needs are like the
promise of the plant that is easy to cultivate with
nutritionally complete food in the seed that stores well,

Table 3. Principal Leafy Vegetables Used as Food in the Humid Tropics With Potential for Further Improvement

Genus/Species	Common Name	Area Where Cultivated and Used
(a) Annual hot season leafy vegetables		
Amaranthus spp.	Amaranth	
Ipomoea quatica Forsk. (Syn. l. reptans (L.) Poir)	kangkong, water spinach	Southeast Asia and South India
Corchorus olitorius L.	Jew's mallow jute mallow jute	Originated in Southern China and taken to Indian sub-continent
Xanthosoma brasiliense (Desf.) Engler. Xanthosoma sagittifolium (L.) Schott.	calalou, yautia cocoyan	Both originated in tropical South America, X. brasiliense now mainly cultivated in South America, Caribbean and Pacific for its leaves, while X. sagittifolium is pantropical

Basella rubra L. (syn. B. alba L.)	Ceylon spinach Malabar night-shade	Origin South Asia or South America, now pantropical
Solanum macrocarpon L. Solanum acthiopicum L. Solanum incanum L.	African eggplant	All three Solanum spp. originated in Africa and are cultivated there
Solanum nigrum L.	Black nightshade	Native region unknown. At present a cosmopolite weed which is cultivated
Talinum triangulare (Jacq.) Willd.	Water leaf, talinum	Originated probably Central and/or South America or Tropical Africa. Cultivated in Brazil, West Indies and West Africa
Celosia argentea L.	quail grass sokoyoloto	
Hibiscus sabdariffa L.	Roselle	Originated in Africa, now grown to a large extent in the drier parts of West and Central Africa and India

Table 3. (cont'd)

Genus/Species	Common Name	Area Where Cultivated and Used
(b) Annual cool season leafy vegetables		
Brassica campestris L. spp. chinensis (L.) Makino	pak-choi	Asia Pantropical
Brassica campestris ssp. pekinensis (Lour.) Rupr.	Chinese cabbage	Asia Pantropical
Brassica juncea (L.) Gran. & Coss.	Chinese mustard	Asia Pantropical
Brassica carinata A. Br.	Ethiopian mustard	Asia Pantropical
Brassica oleracea L.	Cabbage, kale	Asia Pantropical
Lactuca sativa L.	lettuce	Primary center of L. sativa in the Middle East and of L.

Lactuca indica L.	Indian lettuce	indica in India, Japan, Philippines where it is cultivated. L. sativa is more popular in Latin America, Africa and the Near East than in India and Southeast Asia.
Beta vulgaris var. cicla L.	Swiss chard	Originated in the Mediterranean area and becoming increasingly popular in cool tropical areas as a vegetable
(c) Perennial vegetables		
Moringa oleifera Lam.	Drumstick tree horseradish tree	Originated in India, very popular there and in Southeast Asia and West Africa
Veronia amygdalina Delile	Bitter leaf	Originated in tropical Africa. Popular vegetable in West Africa. Other wild or cultivated Veronia species are known in tropical lowlands of Asia, Africa and America.
Cnidoscolus chayamansa McVaugh	chaya, tree spinach	Grown in compounds in the Caribbean area and Central America

Table 3. (cont'd)

Genus/Species	Common Name	Area Where Cultivated and Used
Sauropus androgynus Merr.	sauropus	Grown in India, Malaysia, and Indonesia as a leaf vegetable in home gardens
Abelmoschus manihot (L.) Medik.	aibika	India, Pakistan, through Southern China to New Guinea and North Australia. Widely grown in Pacific Islands

(d) Leaves of food crops grown for other purposes

Manihot esculenta Crantz.	cassava	Cassava originated in Central and South America. Secondary gene centers almost certainly exist in Africa. Cassava leaves are consumed in many countries, especially in West Africa, Indonesia, Malaysia and parts of South America

Ipomoea batatas (L.) Lam.	sweet potato	Originated in Central and Northern South America, now pantropical. The leaves are used as potherbs in Southeast Asia, the Pacific, and Latin America
Colocasia esculenta (L.) Schott	taro	Originated in Indo-Malaysia. Spread eastwards and westwards, now pantropical
Vigna unguiculata (L.) Walp.	cowpea yardlong bean	Primary center West and Central Africa. Introduced into the Indian subcontinent where ssp. sequipedalis (L.) Verdc. (Yardlong bean) developed. The leaves of both cowpea and yardlong bean are frequently consumed and in West and Central Africa cowpeas are traditionally grown purely as a leaf vegetable

Source: D.H. van Sloten, 1981. Changing priorities - the genetic resources of leafy vegetables. Paper presented at FAO/UNEP/IBPGR Technical Conference April 1981 Rome. 13 p. mimeo.

Table 4. Principle Fruits used as Vegetables in the Humid Tropics with Potential for Further Improvement

Genus/Species	Common Name	Area Where Cultivated and Used
Cucurbits		
Most are of low nutritional composition with the exception of the yellow-fleshed pumpkins and mellons which possess a high B-carotene content and the bitter gourd (widely consumed in South Asia) which has a high iron and vitamin C content. The daily intake of cucurbits may be very high in certain parts of the tropics, so although they are not nutrient dense their contribution of daily vitamins and minerals should not be underestimated. In addition, several of the cucurbits listed below are cultivated for their mature seed (long after the fruit is suitable as a fleshy vegetable) which are rich in protein and oil and by weight are comparable to peanuts and soybeans.		
Trichosanthes cucumerina L.	snake gourd (young and ripe fruits)	Indo-Malaysian
Citrullus lanatus (Thunb.) Mansf.	watermelon	Pantropical (African)
Cucumis melo L.	melon, muskmelon, cantaloupe	Pantropical (Near East)
Cucumis sativus L.	cucumber, gherkin	Pantropical
Cucumis anguria L.	West Indian gherkin, squashes, vegetable marrow	Tropical Americas

Benincasa hispida (Thunb.) Cong.	waxgourd, white gourd, Chinese preserving melon	Chinese/Indo/Malaysia
Coccinia grandis (L.) Voigt	ivy gourd (young and ripe fruits and leaves)	India (Africa)
Lagenaria siceraria (Molina) Standl.	bottle gourd, white flowered gourd	Pantropical
Luffa acutangula (L.) Roxb.	loofah, sponge gourd	Indian
Momordica charantia L.	bitter gourd, calabash	Indian
Sechinum edule (Jacq.) Swartz	chayote, guisquil	MesoAmerica
Cyclanthera pedata (L.) Schrad.	korila (young and ripe fruits and shoots)	Tropical America

Leguminous Vegetables

Used fresh with significant vitamin, mineral and protein content. The long-lasting or perennial, climbing, deep-rooting tropical leguminous vegetables such as lima bean, winged bean, hyacinth bean and yardlong bean together with the non-climbing pigeon pea, are valuable plants for home garden production since they are less susceptible to diseases, are often more water and soil tolerant and by their climbing and shrub like nature can make full use of available space and light of small garden plots.

Phaseolus vulgaris L.	common bean	Pantropical (Americas)
Phaseolus lunatus L.	Lima bean	Pantropical (Americas)

Table 4. (cont'd)

Genus/Species	Common Name	Area Where Cultivated and Used
Dolichos lablab L. (Lablab niger Medik.)	hyacinth bean	Indian
Vigna radiata (L.) Wilczek	mung bean	S.E. Asia
Vigna unguiculata (L.) Walp	yardlong bean	S.E. Asia
Psophocarpus tetragonolobus (L.) DC.	winged bean	S.E. Asia
Parkia biglobosa Benth.	locust bean	African
Canavalia gladiata (Jacq.) DC.	sword bean	S.E. Asia (Pantropical)
Pachyrrhizus erosus (L.) Urban	yam bean	S.E. Asia
Glycine max (L.) Merr.	soybean	Pantropical (S.E. Asia)
Cajanus cajan (L.) Mill.	pigeon pea	Indian/Asia/Africa
Arachis hypogaea L.	groundnut	Pantropical (S. America)
Voandzeia subterranea (L.) Thou.	Bambara groundnut	African

Pisum sativum L.	garden pea	Temperate crops grown in winter season
Vicia faba L.	broad bean	Temperate crops grown in winter season
Solanaceous Fruits		
Cyphomandra betacea Sendt.	tree tomato	Tropical Americas (S.A.)
Physalis peruviana L.	husk tomato	Pantropical (Americas)
Capsicum spp.	chili peppers	Pantropical
Solanum melongena L.	eggplant	Indian/Pantropical
Solanum macrocarpon L.	African eggplant	African
Other Fruits Used Green as Vegetables		
Moringa oleifera Lam.	drumstick tree (young fruits)	India
Hibiscus esculentus L.	okra	India/Africa
Zea mays L.	sweet corn	Pantropical (Americas)
Mushrooms (like the rice straw)	these are tropical mushrooms	

leaves that can be used as a vegetable, stems that fuel the
fire and roots that bake like bread. Somehow this dream
seems to be universal but the fact remains the best potential new crops are the as yet unused genes in our basic
crops (IBPGR 1979, 1980, 1981).

Conclusion

It is an unfortunate fact that not all useful plants
are discovered before their habitats are destroyed and not
all useful plants once discovered are preserved in their
full genetic diversity. Extinction represents an irreversible loss of a unique resource. Throughout the world,
people increasingly consume food, take medicine and employ
industrial materials that owe their production to genetic
resources. The era of expansion is over and to sustain a
quality of life germplasm conservation has got to be a
societal priority.

The founders of this country clearly recognized the
value of plants in fulfilling the food and fiber needs of
its inhabitants. Thomas Jefferson speaking to the needs of
the new and growing country is quoted as saying, "The
greatest service which can be rendered any country is to add
a useful plant to its culture." The importance of the
contribution today is no less than it was 200 years ago.

The problem of supplying enough food is clearly before
us worldwide. If we take seriously the existence of hunger
and malnutrition that exist now, then food production will
have to increase between three and four-fold worldwide given
the current mal-distribution of food supplies and projected
population increases. To not anticipate change is to be
ill-prepared for the future.

Our increased influence over the environment to
maintain an abundance of food in the face of an increasing
population has decreased our margin for error. It is
clearly in our national interest to maintain a strong agricultural research program to insure attention to the conservation, evaluation and open distribution of crop plant
germplasm. Without this foundation there will be little
potential for future crop plant enhancement.

Literature Cited

AAAS. 1981. Recommendations of the Genetic Engineering
     Expert Panel. Ad hoc Genetic Engineering Panel of the
     American Association for the Advancement of Science,
     Washington, D.C.

Abelson P.H. ed. 1975. Food: Politics, Economics, Nutrition and Research. Am. Assoc. Adv. Science. Washington, D.C. 202 pp.

CEQ. 1981. Global Future: Time to Act. Council on Environmental Quality. Washington, D.C. 209 pp.

CIAT. 1980. Beets program annual report for 1979. Calli Columbia. 79 pp.

CIMMYT. 1980. Review. Centro Intern. de Mejoramiento de Maiz y Trigo. Mexico D.F. 100 pp.

Cooper, I.P. 1980. The Patent System and the "New Biology". Rutgers Journal of Computers, Technology and the Law. 8: 1-46.

Dodds, K.S. 1963. The origins of fruits and vegetables. Span. 6: 64-67.

Eckholm, E. 1978. Disappearing Species: The Social Challenge. World Watch Paper 22. Worldwatch Institute, Washington, D.C. 38 pp.

FAO. 1976. Production Year Book 1975, Vol. 29. FAO Rome.

FAO. 1981. Agriculture: Toward 2000. Food and Agriculture Organization, Rome. 134 p. + statistical annex xxv.

Forum. 1983. Report of the 1982 Plant Breeding Research Forum. Pioneer Hi-Bred Intern. Inc. Des Moines. 237 pp.

Frankel, O.H. 1967. Guarding the plant breeders' treasury. New Scientist 35: 538-540.

_____. 1974. Genetic conservation; our evolutionary responsibility. Genetics 78: 53-65.

_____, and Bennet, E., eds. 1970. Genetic Resources in Plants — their exploration and conservation. Blackwell Oxford and Edinborough. IBP Handbook No. 11. 538 pp.

_____, and Hawkes, J.G., eds. 1975. Genetic Resources — for today and tomorrow. Cambridge University Press, Cambridge. 492 pp.

_____, and Soule, M. 1981. Conservation and Evolution. Cambridge University Press, Cambridge. 327 pp.

Grubben, G.J.H. 1977. Tropical vegetables and their genetic resources In: H.D., Tindall and J.T., Williams eds AGPE: IBPGR 77/23. Intern. Board Plant Genetic Resources. Rome.

Harlan, J.R. 1971. Agricultural origins: centers and non-centers. Science 174: 468-474.

_____. 1975. Our vanishing genetic resources. Science 188: 618-622.

Hernandez-X, E. 1970. Exploracion Ethnobotanica y Su Metodologia. Escuela Nac. de Agricultura Mexico. 69 pp.

Hodge, W.H., and C.O. Erlanson. 1956. Federal Plant Introduction — A Review. Economic Botany 10: 299-334.

IBPGR. 1979. A Review of Policies and Activities 1974-78 and of the prospects for the Future. International Board for Plant Genetic Resources, Rome. FAO/IBPGR 78/24. 128 pp.

IBPGR Annual Report. 1980. International Board for Plant Genetic Resources, Rome. 103 pp.

_____. 1981. The IBPGR in the Eighties: A Strategy and Planning Report. International Board Plant Genetic Resources. FAO/IBPGR 80/32. 29 pp.

Iltis, H.H. 1981. The National Science Foundation, the Reagan Administration and wild green tomatoes. Manuscript. 15 pp.

IUCN. 1980. World Conservation Strategy. International Union for the Conservation of nature and Natural Resources, Gland, Switzerland.

Jensen, N.F. 1962. First world gene bank. Crops and Soils 15: 14-15.

Klose, N. 1950. America's Crop Heritage. Iowa State College Press. 156 pp.

Lappé, F.M. and Collins, J. 1979. Exploding the Hunger Myths. Institute for Food and Development Policy. San Francisco. 30 pp.

Mooney, P.R. 1980. Seeds of the Earth. Canadian Council for International Cooperation (Ottawa) and the International Coalition for Development Action (London). 126 pp.

NAS. 1972. Genetic Vulnerability of Major Crops. National Academy of Science, Washington, D.C. 307 pp.

_____. 1975. Underexploited tropical plants with promising eocnomic value. Washington, D.C. 186. pp.

_____. 1978. Conservation of Germplasm Resources: An Imperative. Washington, D.C. 118 pp.

_____. 1979. Tropical Legumes: Resources for the Future. Washington, D.C. BOSTID. 331 pp.

_____. 1980. Conversion of Tropical Moist Forest. Washington, D.C. 205 pp.

NAS. 1982. Ecological Aspects of Development in the Humid Tropics. National Academy of Science. Washington, D.C. 297 pp.

Myers N. 1983. A Wealth of Wild Species. Westview Press, Boulder. 274 pp.

Prescott-Allen, R., and C. Prescott-Allen. 1981. In Situ Conservation of Crop Plant Resources, a report to the International Board for Plant Genetic Resources by the International Union for the Conservation of Nature and Natural Resources. Gland, Switzerland. 145 pp.

Reitz, L. 1976. Improving germplasm resources. In: Germplasm Resources, Am. Soc. Agron., Madison, Wis. 97 pp.

Ruthenberg, H. 1976. Farming Systems in the Tropics. Clarendon Press, Oxford. 366 pp.

Singleton, W.R. and D.F. Jones. 1938. Linkage relations of O_1, O_2. Maize Gen. Coop. News Letter 4: 4.

Thompson, P.A., and Brown, G.E. 1972. The seed unit at the Royal Botanic Gardens. Kew Bulletin 20: 445-456.

U.S. Government Agricultural Research Policy Advisory Committee. 1973. Recommended Actions and Policies for Minimizing the Genetic Vulnerabilities of Our Major Crops. USDA and National Association of State

Universities and Land Grant Colleges, Washington, D.C. 33 pp.

U.S. Government. 1979. Plant Genetic Resources: Conservation and Use. Prepared by National Plant Genetic Resources Board. U.S. Government Printing Office, 1979. 280-931 SEA-124. 20 pp.

USDA. 1981. The National Plant Germplasm System. Science and Education. U.S. Department of Agriculture, Washington, D.C. (various page numbers.)

Vavilov, N.I. 1926. Studies on the Origin of Cultivated Plants. Institute of Applied Botany and Plant Breeding, Leningrad.

Wilkes, G. 1977. The World's Crop Plant Germplasm — an Endangered Resource. Bulletin of Atom. Sci. 33: 8-16.

Wilkes, G. 1983. Current Status of Crop Plant Germplasm. CRC Reviews in Plant Sciences 1: 133-181.

_____, and Wilkes, S.K. 1972. The Green Revolution. Environment 14: 32-39.

Whyte, R.O. and Julen, G. 1963. Proceedings of a technical meeting on plant exploration and introduction. FAO, Genetica Agraria 17: 1-573.